W9-DGS-712

The Great Garbo

The
Great
Garbo

Robert Payne

Cooper Square Press

First Cooper Square Press edition 2002

This Cooper Square Press hardcover edition of *The Great Garbo* is an unabridged republication of the edition first published in New York in 1976. It is reprinted by arrangement with the Estate of Robert Payne.

Copyright © 1976 by Robert Payne
Originally published in 1976 by Praeger Publishers

Published by Cooper Square Press
A Member of the Rowman & Littlefield Publishing Group
200 Park Avenue South, Suite 1109
New York, New York 10003-1503
www.coopersquarepress.com

Distributed by National Book Network

A previous edition of this book was cataloged as follows by the Library of Congress:

Payne, Pierre Stephen Robert, 1911–1983
    The great Garbo

    Filmography: p.
    Bibliography: p.
    Includes index.
    1. Garbo, Greta, 1905– I. Title.
    ISBN 0-8154-1223-1 (cloth alk.paper)

PN2778.G3P37
791.43'028'0924 [B]

73–11784

♾™ The paper used in this publication meets the minimum requirements of American National Standard for Information Sciences—Permanence of Paper for Printed Library Materials, ANSI/NISO Z39.48–1992.
Manufactured in the United States of America.

For
Patricia
amantissima diva

Contents

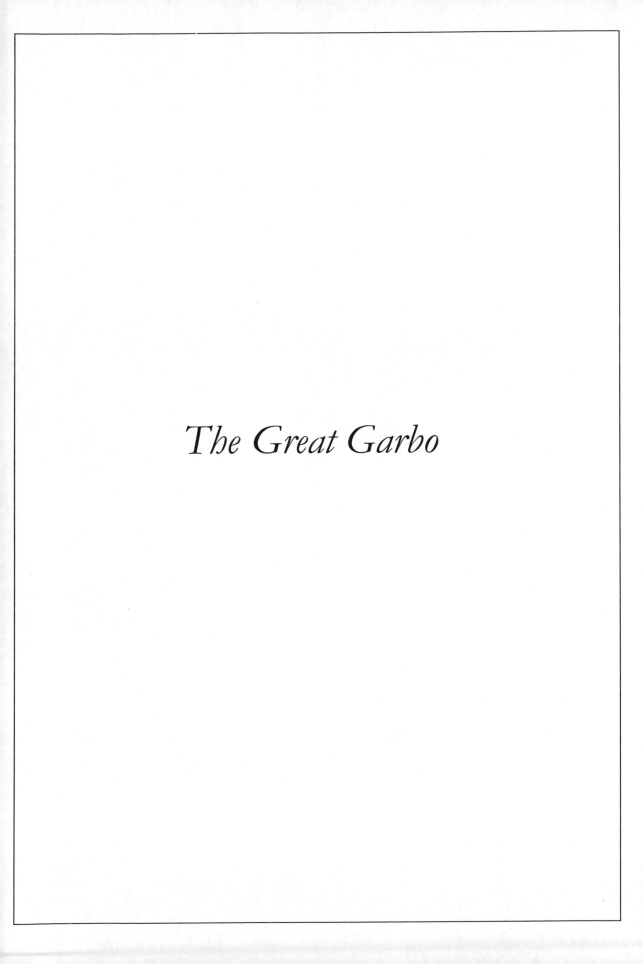

The Great Garbo

The Legend

> What if man had eyes to see perfect
> beauty—I mean the divine beauty,
> pure and clear and unsullied by the
> corruptions of mortality and by all
> the colors and vanities of human
> life—what if man could look upon
> and hold converse with perfect
> beauty in its divine simplicity?
> —PLATO, *The Symposium*

SHE ALONE AMONG the women of her time became a legend. She lived her earthly life more or less conventionally, was recognizably human, said the things expected of her, but as a legend she swept out of ordinary human life altogether and was loved and adored by millions of people for no reason except that in their eyes she deserved their love and adoration. She was not, except rarely, a great actress. She had no message. She made no speeches, led no movements, and did not, like Helen of Troy, walk along the battlements of a city about to be conquered while everyone watched her. Her life was singularly uneventful. But the legend grew, feeding on her beauty. A century from now people will still be talking about the perfect beauty of her face.

It was a face to make the gods envious: a face of the utmost refinement, chiseled in cold steel, purified in roaring fires, smooth as a pebble in a mountain stream, and so beautiful that it was almost frightening in the intensity of its beauty. Here was the divine beauty, of which Plato spoke and poets have dreamed. Almost she was the abstraction of beauty, a Platonic ideal, remote and unreal, yet remaining undeniably present, casting a spell on all who saw her.

It was a strange phenomenon, never repeated—a face whose outlines were perfect from every angle. You could walk around it and study it, and every moment would reveal a new perfection. Nose, chin, mouth, cheeks, forehead—all were in perfect balance. Her features were dominated by large, glowing eyes, which were alive with an inner light, so that it seemed possible to converse with her without uttering a word, simply by observing and responding to the continually changing light in her eyes. Her eyelids were heavy, and her lashes were unusually long. Once, when a friend wondered aloud whether the eyelashes were real, she said, "Pull them—you'll see!" So they were pulled, and it was observed that they really belonged to her. When she appeared in public she painted them with mascara. Without mascara they had the same color as her fair hair.

No other actress resembled her, for she resembled no one. She possessed to an extraordinary degree the quality of being memorable, and this was due not only to her beauty but also to the urgent life flowing through her face—a wild, childlike enthusiasm that seemed to lie just below the surface of her skin. Her movements had the quickness of a child's movements; she smiled almost too quickly, as children do; and when she walked she strode like a conqueror, as children often do. She laughed as a child laughs, shook her shoulders as a child does, and gave herself freely, holding nothing back. And if in movement she was childlike, she had, when quite still, the bearing of a Queen or an Empress. She was quite conscious that she possessed this imperial quality, but because she was equally beautiful whether smiling or frowning or being imperious, no one could possibly take offense. Her beauty was continually getting in the way of her acting, because audiences rarely cared what emotions she was portraying in those many films that were totally unworthy of her. For them she was more a goddess than an actress.

The most wonderful thing about her was the radiance that streamed from her face, like a calm, white, pure, transparent light. So Aphrodite must have looked when she came fresh from the sea with the salt spray still clinging to her. The radiance was dazzling. In an age that had seen no goddesses walking the earth, people instinctively recognized that, if she was not a goddess, she was as close to being one as any mortal can be. In her glance there was always more of blessing than command, and there was often astonishment, as though she had not quite accustomed herself to being adored. She was at once childlike, virginal, queenly, and maternal, possessing therefore that contradictory set of qualities demanded of supreme goddesses, together with the perfect beauty that is also demanded of them.

She came at a time when she was most needed, in the troubled years

following World War I, and she vanished forever from the screen in the early months of World War II. She came into a world that had been expecting her or at least hoping that a goddess would appear, and she came armed with all the weapons of a goddess. Power, majesty, splendor —all those things that are almost beyond the range of human aspiration —seemed to be hers by natural right. She could enslave men with a smile or destroy them with a glance. Women were not jealous of her, because she was so much more beautiful than they would ever dare to be; men did not desire her, because she was clearly beyond the reach of human desire, even though on the screen she went through the motions of love-making. Her screen lovers looked ridiculous; every man thought he could do better and at the same time felt free of any responsibility to prove himself. It was enough to contemplate her beauty, to drown in it. There was something in that face as elemental as the trees, the wind, and carved rocks. Snow became fire; fire became snow again. Somewhere at the heart of the mystery there was a raging volcano.

She was the *stella assoluta*, the star above all other stars. This, too, was an honor accorded to her by divine right; she had not worked for it. She accepted these honors with a simple grace, and though conscious of her beauty, she made light of it. To most people she remained a mystery, but the chief mystery was how anyone could possibly be so beautiful. It was as though God had finally created a face totally without blemish and in the most perfect form He could imagine, rounded and complete. There was something so pure and classical in that face you suspected she had once been stone and would soon turn to stone again; it was inconceivable that she would grow old and inconceivable that she would die.

Her body was of the same texture as her face. It was long and lithe and seemed to need no effort to set it in motion. She did not walk so much as stride with quick panther-like steps. Her shoulders were square and broad, her breasts small, her hips full, her hands long, tapering, and beautifully formed. From shoulders to knees she had the body of an athlete, but she had the legs and feet of a peasant accustomed to heavy labor, all the more beautiful because they were solidly constructed for strength. It was at once the body of a goddess, a child, and a mature woman. Even when she lay voluptuously on bearskins, there was always a hint of the gawky, long-legged child she had been. Like her face, her body sometimes assumed the texture of a stone, became immobile, lost in meditation; and then, as quickly as she smiled, her body leaped into movement. But mostly it remained invisible and unknown. Spellbound by her face, you rarely found yourself looking at her lithe, young body. In the enchantment of her smile all desire was stilled.

Her body, indeed, scarcely existed for audiences. They were aware

that it moved across a room, that it was well and properly fashioned, and that it would sometimes fall into the arms of a screen lover. But she existed more powerfully in close-up, when her body was cut off, as though it did not exist. She existed as a face and a presence. When Homer sought to convey an image of Helen, he spoke of her walking along the ramparts of Troy wearing a shining veil, but he never described her face. It was enough for the Greeks to see the shining veil to guess at the prodigious beauty beneath. Nor was it necessary to describe Garbo; she, too, wore a shining veil, and her beauty both concealed and revealed her. Her strangeness became familiar, but she was nonetheless strange. There was always the sense of *déjà vu*. We had all seen her before, but where? In a dream? Or long ago? It was a face glimpsed briefly in a crowd and never forgotten, or remembered in a story told long ago. Or perhaps we had seen her in another life. If we had not seen her, how could we explain the sense of familiarity, the knowledge that she had always been there?

No other woman of the screen had that strange effect on us. Ambiguities crowded around her. She was both remote and very near. She was of this earth, but she was also in a curious way above and beyond the earth. We saw her with the shock of recognition that came to Dante when he encountered Beatrice on the Ponte Vecchio, and at the same time, like Dante, we recognized that we had seen her before, not once but many times. On the screen we watched her playing the role of a *femme fatale*, seductress and temptress, and we knew she was none of these things. We asked ourselves what would happen if the tigress was let loose from her cage? What would happen if they gave her roles worthy of her? In the end, of course, they gave her Queen Christina, Camillè, and Anna Karenina, and these *were* worthy of her, or very nearly worthy of her. But why were so many years spent in a wilderness of silly films? Of her beauty and her talent no one appeared to have the least doubt. Yet year after year she appeared in films that today seem totally absurd and irrelevant, made tolerable only by her presence, by those occasional moments when whatever was not Garbo was obliterated from men's eyes and she alone was present on the screen, splendidly at ease, endowed with all those additional defenses that are reserved for those who are truly beautiful, so that everything was permitted to her. It was even permitted to her to act in seventh-rate films.

The problem was nearly insoluble in the terms understood by the Hollywood producers. They thought of her as a marketable commodity, like chewing gum. They debated endlessly about sales potentials, formulas, advertising, gimmicks. They found a formula—the *femme fatale*—and it seemed to work. They learned that Garbo's audiences were larger

in Europe than in the United States, but did not make the obvious deduction that she should be making films in Europe. They labeled her "Hollywood property," kept her close at hand, gave her screen lovers from their store of matinee idols, and rarely thought about the problem that confronted them at every turn: her perfect beauty demanded a very particular kind of role. Since her face was poetry, the role needed to be poetic. Since the dimensions of film gave her heroic grandeur, her role needed to be heroic. Since she was by training and instinct a dramatic actress, she needed high drama. Instead, she was cast as a mysterious lady of obscure origins doomed to catch good men in her net and to destroy them. Once the formula was established, it appeared that she would never get away from it.

A beautiful, high-spirited unicorn had entered the garden. The owners of the garden examined her, pondered the various problems raised by her coming, and decided to put a collar around her neck and employ her as a workhorse. She became a workhorse with a difference, for she was still a unicorn.

This was one way of solving the problem, but it was not a desirable way. The surprising thing is that for more than three years MGM simply did not know what to do with her. They put her in ten films that were remarkable only for being unremarkable. The poetry and heroic drama were not in the scripts but in her face. She went through these films like a sleepwalker, obeying the orders of her directors, frustrated and ill at ease, drifting. She was already becoming a legend, but the legend had nothing to do with the quality of her films.

The stumbling block was her beauty, which continually startled with the arrogance of its perfect proportions. It had nothing whatsoever to do with conventional beauty, it could not be made to serve conventional ends, except disastrously, and it asked no questions. It existed in its own right and obeyed its own laws. "What if man had eyes to see perfect beauty?" Plato asked in *The Symposium*, and answered in effect that to see perfect beauty was to see the face of God, an experience as dreadful and terrifying as anything one can imagine. In the first of the *Duino Elegies* Rainer Maria Rilke imagines himself crying out to the angels in despair:

> *Who among the angelic hosts would listen to me*
> *If I were to cry out? Even if one among them*
> *Suddenly pressed me against his heart, I would faint away*
> *In the strength of his being. For beauty is nothing*
> *But the beginning of a terror made scarcely endurable,*
> *And we adore it because it serenely disdains*
> *To destroy us. Every angel is terrible.*

The quality she possessed above all was a terrible beauty, a beauty at once destructive and creative, releasing men from their commonplace worlds and making them yearn for the impossible, healing their wounds only to open them again. By her presence she invited perfection; this, itself, was revolutionary enough. Her beauty was such that it obscured the beauty of other women, but there was so much authority in her beauty that it did not make them resentful. On the contrary, they gloried in it. They gloried, too, in the complex workings of her beauty and the havoc it created in the imaginations of men.

One wishes—because perfect beauty is so rare—that she had lived in an age when sculptors, painters, and poets rather than filmmakers could have celebrated her. Film is one of the least permanent of the arts, and already one of her films, *The Divine Woman*, has perished, for the negative is known to have disintegrated and no prints have been found. In the age of Lorenzo de' Medici the sculptors, painters, and poets celebrated the beauty of Simonetta Vespucci in stone, on canvas, and in print. They saw that perfect beauty was living among them and they owed it to themselves to record it for posterity. So we can see her now in innumerable paintings with that chiseled perfection of features and her crown of honey-colored hair, garlanded with jewels that do not in the least add to her beauty but are made beautiful because they adorn her. Alive, she dominated Florence, and when she died of galloping consumption in her early twenties, her body was carried in triumph through the streets of Florence so that people could look on her for the last time, knowing that this miracle would never be repeated.

Like Simonetta Vespucci, Garbo became a legend in her lifetime but did not always know or understand the laws by which legends come into existence. The MGM publicity department claimed that it invented the legend, but in fact the legend had little enough to do with the inventions. She created it herself, almost unconsciously and without effort, when she performed for the first time on the sloping roof of a shed in a shabby courtyard of Stockholm when she was about eight years old. Thereafter, step by step, she became the companion of the legend that walked beside her. She was shy, unruly, capricious, and so terribly insecure that she never realized how much love and affection were contained in the great wave of adoration that engulfed her. Her beauty puzzled her and sometimes frightened her, and was so close and familiar to her that she made light of it. Sometimes she seemed to be a refugee from her own beauty, her own legend, her own loneliness.

Between two wars, in an age of tyrannies, poverty, and massacres, she was one of the few who gave dignity to people's lives. Because she acted out of a full heart and was perfectly beautiful, she came like a divine

grace that arrived unexpectedly and just as unexpectedly vanished away. But though she vanished she was not forgotten. New generations arose to be enchanted, bewildered, and bemused by her. They flocked to the Garbo festivals or looked at her silent films, asking themselves how it was possible for an actress to be so misused by so many directors. And there were many other questions: Why did she permit herself to be misused? And how did it come about that in *Queen Christina* and *Camille* she rose triumphantly over the absurdities that threatened to destroy her as an actress? Why did she abandon films? What did she possess that actors no longer possess? For assuredly she possessed something very strange and rare, and it was not only her beauty.

All people are nests of secrets, and we shall not uncover all the secrets that gathered about Garbo. She reveled in her privacy, lived for her acting, and rejected as far as possible the public rewards of fame. She never said she wanted to be alone. She said she wanted to be let alone, to live her own life. She wanted above all to be a person in her own right, and she realized very early that actors, by the nature of their craft, are likely to become what the public wants them to become. The public threatened to imprison her in its own image of her, and she sensibly drew back sharply in order to save herself. What she had to say had been said in her films; the rest was silence. But the films, when studied closely, sometimes reveal very nakedly the passions of her mind and her astonishing capacity to impose her own moods and thoughts on a story that was necessarily not concerned with her moods and thoughts. She had the power to bend directors, cameramen, actors, and script writers to her will. Sometimes, in the middle of a film, we are aware for a few moments that she is saying something that has nothing to do with the story, which is herself speaking alone and which is more haunting and more memorable than any of the lines written for her.

So this is a portrait of Garbo the actress, her triumphs and her failures, and the unpredictable accidents that brought her to Hollywood and to world fame, so that she became within the space of a few years the star of stars, *stella assoluta*, the one actress of her time who is likely to be remembered in the far distant future.

The Childhood
of Greta Gustafsson

My affection for Sweden is un-
bounded, for the phantoms are
everywhere.
                —RAINER MARIA RILKE

SWEDEN IS A harsh country where the long winters drive out the
memory of the brief summers. A land of blue lakes, desolate mountains,
and interminable forests, with fierce winds racing down from the Arctic,
it has shaped the minds and characters of the people, who are by turns
silent, brooding, exultant, joyous, deeply introspective, and wildly extro-
verted. They are a people of great physical beauty, blue-eyed and flax-
en-haired, with a curious whiteness to their skins, loving life and laughter under the sun, hating those long winters which imprison them in ice
and mist.

   In those long winters the ghosts of the past arise to torment the
modern Swedes. They remember when all northern Europe trembled
before the Swedish sea raiders and the earlier mythological time when
heroic battles were fought in the forests against armies of monsters, and
strange beasts came out of the sea, and the mysterious King Erik made a
village maiden his Queen; and then there were the more recent kings like
Gustavus Vasa, who was murderous and gentle by turns, as he welded a
single kingdom out of scattered tribes, and Gustavus Adolphus, who
welded kingdoms into an empire, raged against the rising power of Mus-

covy, and made good use of his executioners, who wielded thin-bladed axes and wrapped their victims in spiked chains, thus bleeding them to death—the axes and the chains are preserved in the museum on the Götengaten in Stockholm. One Swedish King, Gustavus III, was shot to death in his box in the theatre. Other kings died insane or fell in battle. It was a tempestuous and legendary history worthy of a high-spirited people.

They were also a patient and God-fearing people, who kept records faithfully and wanted their names to be known to posterity. Village muster rolls, baptismal and marriage registers, and burial records were carefully preserved by a people that cherished its past. We know the histories of quite obscure families. We know for example that there was born in the year 1600 in the village of Asby in the province of Östergötland in southeast Sweden a boy who was called Jonas Anderson-Ekstrand. At fifteen he joined the army of Gustavus Adolphus and at thirty returned to his village to marry, having never risen above a common soldier. His wife bore him five sons, and his eldest son, Carl, gave him four grandchildren. Normally the eldest grandchild would have the name Carlsson. For some unknown reason he took the name of Carl Gustaf Frederiksson instead, and his son took the name of Johan Gustafsson. There the bewildering changing of names came to an end, and the children of Johan retained the Gustafsson name. So it came about that in the twelfth generation following Jonas Anderson-Ekstrand there was born in the wretched working-class district of Södermalm in Stockholm a girl called Greta Lovisa Gustafsson, descended from the soldier of Asby and generations of farmers. The world knows her as Greta Garbo.

Stockholm is a city of islands joined by bridges. In the autumn Lake Mälar turns dark and the clouds gather in great white sheets like ice floes. Then the pinnacles and towers of the old city gleam with frost, and when the snow comes the lake is almost as white as the city. At the beginning of winter come sudden chilling rains and clammy mists, and sometimes ferocious winds spin among the islands at seventy miles an hour. Södermalm, built on a rocky island with steep bluffs, is the most exposed part of all. The bluffs trap the wind and send it whistling down the dark, shabby streets. Södermalm belongs to those who have chosen to defy the elements or cannot afford to live elsewhere. It looks down on the lake, the old city, and the bustling harbor; at night you can stand on top of a bluff and look at the lights of the old city in the distance and feel as though you were eternally separated from the real heart of Stockholm.

Things are better now, but in those days penury dogged Södermalm. Mostly it was inhabited by common laborers and small shopkeepers.

The Childhood of Greta Gustafsson

There were a few good streets, and the best was the Götgatan, which cuts straight across the island and has museums, monuments, theatres, and restaurants. It was wide and well-paved, and the shopkeepers took care that the shopfronts were clean and freshly painted. In the side streets it was quite different. Halfway down the Götgatan comes the Blekingegatan with its four- and five-story apartment houses, all ugly. In a small three-room apartment at Blekingegatan 32, on the fourth floor, Greta Lovisa spent most of her childhood. She had been born in the early morning of September 18, 1905, at the local hospital.

Her father, Carl Alfrid Gustafsson, was born in the small village of Frinnaryd in southern Sweden and had spent the first twenty years of his life on his father's farm. He was a handsome man, over six feet tall, and in the surviving photographs his features strongly resemble those of his famous daughter, for they shared the same forehead, eyes, delicately carved nose, and sculptured lips. He had an open and rather sensitive face and did not in the least look like a farmer's son. Indeed, there were people who wondered aloud whether he came from a higher social class. There was something princely about him. He had a good voice and enjoyed singing; he liked reading to his children; he walked gracefully; and there was in him an innate gentleness and kindliness that set him apart from other laborers. He described himself as a machinist, but in fact he spent most of his working life in Stockholm as a common laborer, and life was always difficult for him.

Carl Alfrid was twenty-seven when he married Anna Lovisa Karlsson, a peasant's daughter from the village of Högsby in Värmland in central Sweden. She had a trace of Lapp blood in her ancestry, which was shown in her eyelids, with their Mongolian folds. She was a sensible, bustling, red-cheeked woman, who spoke all her life in a peasant dialect. Unlike her husband, who enjoyed reading, she never read a book, and she spoke very little, not because she was reserved but because she preferred action to words; her warmth and sweet temper were well known to her neighbors. There were two other children in the family: Sven, the firstborn, who resembled his father, and Alva, who resembled her mother.

In later years, when Greta Lovisa had become Greta Garbo, she was asked about her childhood memories. She shook her head. "I remember nothing," she answered. "I cannot even remember those first little gifts of dolls and colored wagons." She remembered going to school and hating nearly every moment of it, but it left little impression on her. There were the usual childish escapades. Next door to the apartment lived an embittered old spinster who complained about the children and was suitably punished by having sand and water thrown at her window,

Greta Gustafsson is the girl in the sailor suit, top center

with Greta Lovisa acting as the ringleader of the small gang. From the beginning she was something of a tomboy, played leapfrog, had her own jealously guarded bag of marbles, and liked to think of herself as a boy. "I am the Gustafsson boy," she said when she went to collect a pair of shoes from the local cobbler, and many years later, when she was famous and living in retirement, she would say of herself: "I am a good boy" or "I am a naughty boy," according to her mood.

Neighbors remembered her as a thin, gawky, moonfaced child who grew up too quickly and rarely had enough to eat. Facing the apartment house there was a kind of construction yard, which the children took over after working hours. They saw her playing about in the yard, dancing gravely by herself or clambering along the roof of a wooden shed, which was sometimes used as a stage or a dance floor. They remembered her deep, warm love for her mother and her quiet adoration of her father, and told stories of how visitors to the Gustafsson apartment sometimes caught sight of her, wrapped in an old curtain and gazing at herself in front of a mirror. They said she was shy and nervous, and sometimes bolted under the table when an unfamiliar visitor appeared; then her father would get down on his hands and knees, and play with her, and cajole her, and at last she would emerge from under the table with her small hand around her father's little finger.

They remembered, too, that she was pathetically sensitive, but rarely burst into tears. Her face would freeze with terror when voices were suddenly raised. She liked to meet her father on his way back from work. She would go skipping down the street, very gay, laughing to herself, and the moment she met him she absorbed his mood: if he was gay, she would be gay, but if he was somber, then she would walk beside him as though she wore somberness like a dark cloak; and she imitated his gestures. Like many younger daughters, she loved her father with a fierce intensity.

The family was close-knit, and she was happiest with her brother and sister. With them, when she was quite small, she played theatre. She was stage designer, author, and principal performer. "We all had to dress up in old costumes and do as we were told," Sven recalled. "Usually she liked to play the part of a boy. Sometimes she would say terrible things. She would point to me and say, 'You be the father,' and then to my sister: 'You be the mother.' Then I would ask her what part she was playing, and she would say, 'I am your child who is drowned.'" When Sven was asked whether Greta Lovisa was happy in Södermalm, he answered, "I don't believe she was really happy until she left school. The only time I remember her being happy was when we stayed during the summer in our grandparents' little hotel in Sparreholm. She liked being out in the country, miles and miles from Stockholm."

But the visits to her grandparents were rare, and she spent most of her childhood and early youth at the Blekingegatan apartment and the Catherina grammar school nearby. At a very early age, according to her brother, she was dreaming of the theatre. He said, "Greta was stage-struck long before she saw a stage or knew about the existence of any actresses." One of those who helped to feed her love for the theatre was Agnes Lind, who kept a little tobacconist's shop on the Blekingegatan. Agnes Lind was a kindly woman who collected photographs of stage stars and cut out the drawings that appeared in picture magazines. Greta Lovisa, whom she knew as "Keta," was one of those who were permitted to examine her scrapbook. "Little Keta used to come to my shop nearly every day," she remembered later. "She would pore over my collection of photographs, and I remember one day when she announced to everyone in my shop that she would be as great as Naima Wyfstrand when she was old enough to go on the stage." At that time Naima Wifstrand, a tall, statuesque Nordic beauty, was the reigning star of the Swedish theatre.

A month before her seventh birthday Greta Lovisa went to school. Her school record, covering the period between August 22, 1912, and June 14, 1919, has survived; it shows that her marks for behavior and application were always A for perfect but that her intellectual development during her first three school years was only fair. The school had a rather cumbersome system for grading the pupils. There were five grades: A, a, ab, ba, B, corresponding to perfect, excellent, good, tolerable, hopeless. She received B's consistently for drawing and gymnastics, A's in Christian teaching, and ab's in reading, writing, and needlework. She got a's or ab's in history, science, mathematics, and geography, and she got consistently high marks for penmanship, which is not surprising, because her handwriting has always been bold and clear. Studying her school report we derive the impression of a girl who is bright and even brilliant but is deliberately holding back, rather lazy and without any decided ambition to make a mark as a scholar, not caring. Her former schoolmates remembered that when she was reprimanded for coming late to school, she simply shrugged her shoulders. Once when the teacher reprimanded her, she reminded him curtly that he himself had come late the day before.

She was growing up fast, and a great deal of her energy was obviously being put into growing. At ten she began growing as fast as a beanstalk, and at twelve she had almost reached her full height. A gangling, awkward, long-shanked girl, she liked to sit at the back of the classroom and to confront her teachers with just a suggestion of rebelliousness. Her former school friends remembered her boyish pout and the way her hair got in front of her eyes, and how her square-ended fingers got covered with ink. They remembered too that she was an efficient and accurate marbles player. They called her G.G. or Keta and usually liked her, but she made few close friends except among students who were remarkably handsome or shared her interest in the theatre.

Those were difficult times. She was almost nine years old when World War I broke out, and soon in neutral Sweden rationing began. In those days nearly everyone in Södermalm knew hunger on a diet of bread and potatoes, with butter costing fifteen kronor a pound and meat unprocurable. They were years of tense excitement and the gripping fear that Sweden might be brought into the war. The war was the one interminable subject of conversation, to be discussed at every meal and far into the night. Greta Lovisa was caught up in the fever, and in 1918, when she was twelve, she directed and performed in a play about the war. The props consisted of old furniture, the actors wore the cut-down clothes of their parents, and Greta Lovisa, wrapped in a white sheet, played the role of the Goddess of Peace, solemnly chanting, "Why do people fight? Why do they shed blood?"

One day in the same year she dawdled in the park on her way to school, playing with the squirrels. The church bells struck nine, and she continued to play for some time, dimly realizing that it was already too late for school and she would probably have to find a credible excuse, but none was forthcoming. She abandoned the idea of going to school, squared her shoulders, and decided to go wandering through the Latin Quarter of Stockholm. Someone had told her you could see Italians there, and they made brightly colored balloons, toy soldiers, and little painted villages you could hold in the palm of your hand. It took her till the early afternoon to find the Italians, and when she found them, she struck up a friendship with a balloon maker. She was still talking with the balloon maker when the late afternoon bell rang at the school. Her brother and sister waited for her at the school gates in the hope that she would turn up, and then went home without her. When it grew dark and there was still no sign of her, the police were informed and search parties were sent out. At ten o'clock that night Greta Lovisa wandered dreamily home, trailing a large red balloon. Her father threw his arms around her, and suddenly the balloon she was holding close to her body burst, and she began to cry. To her the most terrible thing that had happened was the bursting of the balloon. She was more distressed by the fate of the balloon than by her own fate the next day when she was called before the class and spanked across the teacher's knee for being absent without cause.

This incident left a serious blemish on her school record, where it is noted that in the half-year ending in June 1918, she was once absent without the permission of the school or of her parents. She never played truant again. Remarkably healthy, she missed going to school only sixteen days during the entire seven years she attended the Catherina grammar school.

Sometimes worse things happened. One night in winter, when it grows dark very early, she went to meet her father on his return from work. There was a heavy mist on Södermalm and snow on the ground, and by the hazy light of a gaslamp bracketed to the wall she saw two men fighting. One of them was a Swedish giant, so huge and powerful that his tall, thin adversary looked like a pygmy in comparison. They were free-swinging their punches, and sweat was pouring down their faces. The tall, thin man was her father. Paralyzed by fear, she watched them without saying anything, until her father fell in the snow and she was suddenly overwhelmed by blind rage. She threw herself on the giant, screaming, "Why are you hitting him? You mustn't do that! Please let him go!" The giant wrenched himself away from her, stared down at her and then at her father, and said, "All right. Your kid is sticking up for you. I'll let you go. Now go away, both of you!" As she walked home with her father, she was sick with fear and humiliation.

She knew her father drank; but so did all Swedish workmen; and when her father came drunk into the house, her mother knew how to deal with him and usually sent the children away until he recovered. There was nothing new in his drunkenness and his occasional brawling fits of temper. What was new was the humiliation of knowing that her father, whom she adored, was weaker than other men and could be beaten and flung down into the snow with impunity. She remembered his pitiful wide-swinging blows and the look on his face as they returned home together. Of all the traumatic events in her life—and there were many—this was perhaps the most terrible, the most difficult to live with.

By this time she was stage-struck beyond recovery. She was eleven years old when she saw her first stage play, having slipped into the theatre with a free ticket. "It was the greatest thing I had ever seen in my life," she said later. "For me it was like the gates of Heaven opening." With her friend Mona Martenson she began to haunt the stage doors of the Morbakke and Södra theatres on the Götgatan, and announced that she was in love with Carl Pederson, a young ex-boxer who played in musical comedy at the Morbakke and was to become more famous under the name Carl Brisson. Once she steeled herself to thrust some flowers into his hands. He took them gravely, without smiling, and said, "Poor little Keta, go home to your mother." She burst into tears and ran away. On those nights when she wandered up and down the Götgatan, Sven and Alva were sometimes sent out to fetch her home.

The theatre was a refuge, a place of fantasy, an escape from all the humdrum activities of everyday life. She wanted above all to be a stage actress, but there were many obstacles. The greatest obstacle lay in the fact that it was virtually impossible for anyone to go on the stage without passing through the Royal Dramatic Academy, which had been founded by Gustavus III, that extraordinary King who led a revolution against the Estates General, wrote poems and plays that can still be read with pleasure, and showed himself to be the most enlightened of monarchs, for he abolished torture as an instrument of judicial investigation and proclaimed the freedom of the press. Since she was too young and too inexperienced to enter the Royal Dramatic Academy, there remained the possibility of becoming a film actress. Stories were told of people being plucked off the streets to play small roles in films, and there was nothing Greta Lovisa wanted more than to play a small role, or any role. She was not yet twelve when she made her first desperate bid to become a film actress.

One day in February 1917, Greta Lovisa and Mona Martenson set out for the Nordisk film studio on Lidingö Island. They were both tall, handsome, and appealing. They had at one and the same time the awkwardness of children and the appearance of maturity. Greta Lovisa possessed a cool, classic beauty, an egg-white complexion with a sprinkling of freckles over her nose. Mona Martenson, two inches shorter, had a heart-shaped face, a wide smile, and beautiful eyes. Both of them might be taken for seventeen or eighteen. There was no difficulty in reaching Lidingö Island, for you only had to take the streetcar to the terminal and then pay the toll at the bridge leading directly to the island. But since the lake was thickly covered with ice and they had very little money, and on principle objected to paying the toll, they decided to walk over the ice after they reached the terminal. They scrambled down a steep slope and began to cross the ice. Unfortunately there had been a heavy fall of snow, and they walked across the frozen lake with snow up to their knees. They made slow progress and were exhausted by the time they reached the island and went in search of the studio. They asked everyone they met where the studio was, but no one could tell them. They were hungry and bitterly cold. They agreed that it was impossible to find the studio and they would try again when the weather was warmer and the exact location of the studio had been shown to them on a map. Then they returned across the lake, dragging their feet, conscious of failure.

Then it was school again, and more surreptitious visits to theatres and cinemas. Her collection of photographs of Carl Pederson, some of them autographed, filled a shoebox. Her father warned her against attending theatres with free tickets, but she paid little attention to him. This was her life, and she dreamed of nothing else. She wrote poems to Carl Pederson, which have not survived, but a poem addressed to her favorite schoolteacher, Judith Ronnell, has been discovered. It reads:

> *I wish the sun of happiness will fall*
> *Upon the dearest teacher of them all.*
> *This Christmas Day, dear Mrs. Ronnell, please*
> *Accept with all my heart these good wishes.*

Poems very similar to this appeared in almanacs, but it is likely that Greta Lovisa wrote this poem to her teacher without consulting them and with a full heart. "She was a strangely appealing girl," Judith Ronnell recalled. "She was very careful and attentive at her lessons, but her mind was always on the stage. I remember that when any of the students were scolded, she waited for them in the corridor after class and flung her arms around them. She hated what she thought was injustice."

At thirteen she was filling out, and although plump, she already possessed a remarkable beauty. She wore sailor blouses, combed her hair modestly over her forehead, and wore long skirts that reached below her ankles. She had her mother's good health, did not suffer from head colds as her sister, Alva, did, and was already something of a fanatic for the open air. She especially enjoyed riding on a big blue sled down Helgalund Hill, her hair streaming behind her. More and more she grew to resemble her father. She was a quiet, happy, occasionally moody schoolgirl, hardly to be distinguished from a hundred thousand other schoolgirls in Stockholm, except that she was prettier and more sensitive than most, and wildly ambitious.

The war came to an end, and she was still at school. Her grades during the last half-year were better than ever. There was the usual B for drawing, ba's for gymnastics and home economics, and straight A's for nearly everything else. She was at last demonstrating that she could use her mind, but in June 1919 she left school and never returned.

She spent the long summer holiday with her grandparents in the country, but when she returned to Stockholm, she found the whole family in disarray. Her father was in great pain from a serious kidney ailment.

Because no money was coming in, her mother, Alva, and Sven went out
to work, while Greta Lovisa nursed her father and accompanied him on
his weekly visits to the hospital. She was inseparable from him. It was a
long lingering illness, and she watched him die inch by inch. For the first
time she became aware of death, not as an event told in the newspapers
but as something very intimate, growing day by day, oppressively close
to her and inexorable in its progress. His slow death terrified her and left
her emotionally drained. In later years she sometimes talked about the
months spent by her father's bedside as though they were the worst she
had ever lived through, as though her own life came to an end while she
was watching him die.

Winter came, the influenza epidemic swept through Sweden, people
died like flies, and still her father clung to life. It was difficult to live
even with the money earned by her mother and her brother and sister.
That winter the Salvation Army opened soup kitchens for the poor in
Södermalm. When Greta Lovisa was famous, the Salvation Army
officers searched back in their memories and remembered putting on an
entertainment for the children of Blekingegatan. The children themselves
were invited to perform an oriental fantasia as part of the entertainment.
Greta Lovisa wrapped herself in a velvet curtain and assumed the role of
a Chinese princess, holding a fan in her hand and singing strange songs
about an imaginary China. Afterward, with the advantage of hindsight, a
Salvation Army colonel said, "I knew there was a great actress in her as
soon as she appeared on the stage."

No one else knew it; nor indeed in her wildest dreams could Greta
Lovisa have known how soon she would be acclaimed as an actress. In
that miserable winter her thoughts were concentrated on her father and
the ceremonies of sickness and death. He lingered on through the spring
and died on June 1, 1920, at the age of forty-eight. The family, always
close-knit, now became more close-knit than ever.

With the death of her father, something died in Greta Lovisa, and
poverty made her ambition keener. Her childhood and youth were over;
almost she became a mature woman. Less than two weeks after her
father's death she took her first Communion at the Catherina Church
nearby, and a Communion photograph was taken. She rests a plump
elbow on the arm of a high-backed chair, wears a white ankle-length
dress, carries a bouquet of white roses, and decorates her hair with an
enormous white silk bow; and seeing that rather plump face with the
clear eyes and the full lips, you would have said that no experience had
ever touched her, that she would inevitably marry and produce children
and settle down to a comfortable domesticity, and that nothing more

Greta Gustafsson in confirmation dress, June 13, 1920

would ever be heard of her. But the Communion photograph is misleading, for there exist photographs taken earlier that already hint at the mature actress with the clear, chiseled features. Almost it is as though she is playing the role of sweet-faced innocent in the Communion portrait. She wears a mask—it is the mask that used to appear on chocolate boxes. She wears it well, but it is not altogether convincing. The lips are a little too full, the eyes are a little too large, the bang over her forehead is a little too artfully displayed, and we are left with the impression that she is doing what all aspiring actresses must learn to do: she is improving on her beauty with make-up, eye shadow, and the refinements of the hairdresser.

With the death of her father and her first Communion, her childhood came to an end. She was fourteen. Within two years she would make her first film, and three years later she would become a star. Her life was about to speed up prodigiously.

Years later, when there was hardly anyone in America or Europe who had not fed on her beauty and marveled at the subtle contours of her face, the inevitable interviewers asked her about her parents and her childhood. Her face reddened with anger. "Why should I tell you? What business is it of yours?" She went on to declare that she had a right to total privacy, and she was not in the least inclined to answer their questions. She said, "Some people were born in red brick houses, others in plain white board ones. What is the difference? We were all born in houses. I will not have it pointed out that I was born in this house or that; that my mother was this, or my father is that. They were my mother and my father. Why should the world talk about them? I don't want the world to talk about my mother and my father."

Yet the world, which admired her acting and her beauty, was entitled to some knowledge of her. She did not spring out of nowhere. Her vast popularity came about as the result of causes intimately related to her life; and if the press agents were responsible for a part of her popularity, there were other reasons why she appealed so deeply to men and was regarded by women with affection and despair. In spite of her beauty, both men and women felt a kinship with her. She belonged to them; she became familiar to them; she filled their dreams. She was, or seemed to be, all that women wanted to be and all that men desired. She brought to the screen something new and yet familiar, something that people instinctively recognized. It was not an accident that the two giants of the screen were Greta Garbo and Charlie Chaplin; they had much more in common than is usually perceived.

When she said, "What business is it of yours?" she was defending her-

The Childhood of Greta Gustafsson

self against relentless invasions of her privacy. She did not want it to be known that she had grown up in poverty and that her childhood had often been miserable. Once she had been a barefoot waif who dreamed up fantastic characters to play in a windswept yard, standing on the low roof of a shed while she declaimed passages of childish poetry. Like all those who have seen misery, she was secretive. It was as though she was trying to say, "I will not tell you who my father was, because if I told you there would be no secrets left to me." The shadow of her father lay over her. To the very end, and throughout all her screen roles, there could be detected in the strange beauty of her face the knowledge of tragedy.

The Coming of Garbo

Garbon: A mysterious sprite that sometimes comes out at night to dance to the moonbeams.

THE WINTER of 1919 dragged on, and spring was late in coming. With the war over, there poured into Sweden more wealth than men had ever known before. By the summer it was the richest country in Europe, with the iron mines and lumber mills working overtime, and the slipways in the shipyards were full of men building ships. Investors were pouring money into the growing film industry, which could hardly absorb the magnificent sums placed at the disposal of a handful of brilliant directors. Characteristically the film studios were turning out full-length epics on the glories of medieval Sweden.

At this time Swedish filmmaking was dominated by two extraordinary directors: Victor Sjöström and Mauritz Stiller. Sjöström was Swedish, and Stiller was a Russian Jew from Finland. Sjöström was heavily built, calm, philosophic, down-to-earth. Stiller was tall, slender, craggy-faced, and his emotions played on his face as though they were trying to tear him apart. He had bushy hair, heavy eyebrows, a parchment skin, and eyes that blazed like a tiger's. They called him "the big Mauritz," and he gave the impression of a man who was well aware of his genius and would brook no interference. In all this he was justified, for he had a brilliant understanding of film and a wonderful sense of theatricality; in addition he was an excellent violinist and therefore possessed a precise feeling for rhythm. He had been an actor on the legitimate stage, knew the actors' problems, and was capable of going to any lengths to obtain just the quality of acting he desired. He gave promise of becoming one of the greatest film directors of his time.

During 1919 he made his greatest film, *Herr Arnes pengar* (*Sir Arne's Treasure*), based on a story by Selma Lagerlöf. It is the story of three Scots mercenaries in the army of Johan III of Sweden who decide to become freebooters, are arrested and thrown into a castle, and escape to take vengeance on the man who imprisoned them. Disguised as wandering tanners in search of work, they march through a deathly winter to Sir Arne's castle, pillage it, set it on fire, and drive off with its treasure, leaving only the orphan girl Elsalill alive. The mercenaries make their way to the seacoast, while Elsalill follows them in her dreams. The horse, the sledge and the treasure vanish without a trace while they are marching across the thin ice of a lake. Elsalill takes refuge in a fish merchant's hut; she has second sight, knows where they are and what will happen to them. One night she finds herself being mysteriously led toward the inn where the mercenaries are staying, and against all reason she falls in love with Sir Archie, the leader of the mercenaries. She knows he is guilty of terrible crimes but feels she must protect him even when a chance remark about Sir Arne's treasure leads the innkeeper to summon the soldiers; and when the soldiers come, Sir Archie uses the girl as a human shield while fighting his way through a blizzard to his ship. Elsalill dies with a spear thrust in her heart. The mercenaries reach the ship but are betrayed before the shipmaster sets sail. There follows an astonishing and beautiful sequence as the Swedes recover Elsalill's body and the black-robed women follow her cortege across the snow, passing under the prow of the ship.

There are miraculous things in *Sir Arne's Treasure*: the escape of the three freebooters from the castle tower, the burning of Sir Arne's castle, the villagers coming with their buckets of water to put out the flames, the solemn march of the Scots across the snow after they have lost their treasure, their roistering at the inn, and Elsalill's strange dreams and visions. Finally there are the black-robed women in the snow, their very movements expressing the weight of their grief and a terrible pity.

Stiller's film took Stockholm by storm. He employed every trick known to cinema: close-ups, dissolves, masks, superimposed images, sudden changes of tempo—a slow dreamy pace for the visionary scenes and an unbelievably fast pace for the scenes of fighting. At all times he was in complete control. With elegance and an unerring instinct for the exactly right camera angle, with a pervading sense of lyricism, he achieved a masterpiece and showed that the Swedish cinema had come to maturity. The film was tinted, thus giving it a heightened sense of reality. Mary Johnson, who played Elsalill with a beautiful and eerie tenderness, was now regarded as the supreme star of the Swedish cinema. Stiller's early films had shown little understanding of the Swedish temperament, but now at last he had acquired a precise, imaginative understanding of the Swedish mind. He was thirty-six, and at the height of his powers.

Among those who saw the film many times was Greta Lovisa, who saw herself as Elsalill. In the spring of 1920 she made her first attempt to convince Stiller that she was a great actress. One day she waited for him outside the gate of his house, pounced on him when he drove up in an automobile, and begged for a screen test. Stiller looked her up and down, asked a few polite questions, and told her she was altogether too young to be considered as a screen actress. "Come back to me when you have had more experience," he said gently, and then waved her away. He did not forget her. There were to be two more meetings between them before he finally accepted her.

Greta Lovisa was biding her time. She was determined to become an actress, still haunting the theatres and cinemas. She was earning some money as a lather girl in a barber shop. Many barbers in Stockholm have claimed that she worked for them, but only one named Arthur Ekengren, with a shop on the Götgatan, has described her convincingly. He gave her seven kronor a week.

In Sweden the lather girl is an accepted and convenient part of the establishment. She ties the bib round the customer's neck, prepares the lather, pats it on the customer's face, cleans the razor blades, and warms the towels. She talks to the customers about the weather, hands them newspapers from the racks, and receives tips. According to Arthur Ekengren, she was a good lather girl—gay, industrious, popular with his customers. She had a pleasant singing voice, and he remembered her singing arias from Swedish operas. She was always expecting something would "turn up"—it appeared that she had friends in the studios who were looking out for a job for her. In the early morning, when she entered the shop, she would go straight to the cupboard where she kept her white uniform, and one by one she would kiss the seventeen or eighteen portraits of Carl Pederson tacked onto the inside of the cupboard door, and when the shop closed in the evening, she would kiss them again. "For us," Arthur Ekengren said, "she was a ray of sunshine. We never hoped to have a better girl or a more obliging one. She was always happy. There were some days when I really thought she would burst with excitement. She would throw her arms around my wife and

The Coming of Garbo

say she would be a great actress one day, and she dreamed—I have never known anyone who dreamed so much. She would tell us her dreams, and they were all about beautiful princesses who were found by handsome young princes. I can tell you, Keta lived her life to the full, and we all envied her!"

They remembered other things about her: her habit of pirouetting on one leg while stropping a razor, and how once when she was asked, "Why are you laughing?" she answered, "Why isn't everyone laughing?" Her gaiety was infectious. Sometimes she would have all the customers laughing at her stories. She was delighted to be away from school, she was in love with Carl Pederson, and she was going through that happy stage in adolescence when everything in the world is pleasant. She was going regularly to the theatre on her own money, and there were people who complained of her shrill bravos whenever anything happened on the stage that pleased her.

But all this was the outward Greta Lovisa. The inner woman was miserable. After her father died, she did what many people do when they are grief-stricken: she decided to uproot herself and change her life as completely as possible, and so she sent an application for a job in Paul U. Bergström's department store, which faced the Haymarket in the center of Stockholm. The store, usually known as PUB, was famous throughout Sweden. She was interviewed and told that her application would be considered seriously, and within a few days she was working as a packer in the store and earning 125 kronor a month, an unheard of amount of money for her. She began working at Bergström's on July 26, 1920, and continued to work there for two years.

Bergström's keeps its records carefully, and so there can still be seen the application form she filled out: FULL NAME: Greta Lovisa Gustafsson, ADDRESS: Blekingegatan 32, EDUCATION: Catherina, BIRTH: 18/9 1905. The handwriting, as always, was bold and well formed, with large, balanced, decorative capitals, and the letters were neatly joined to each other.

For their files Bergström's also took a photograph of her in a simple black dress, her bobbed hair brushed back from her forehead and puffed up a little at the sides. She smiles tentatively, rather girlishly, and is not yet a raving beauty. She is playing the role of a dutiful and solicitous shopgirl.

At first it was a very humble job, but long before the end of the year she was advanced to the dignity of the Ladies' Coats Department. The floor manager praised her, saying she moved like quicksilver. From Ladies' Coats she was advanced to Ladies' Hats, and the management was so pleased with her services that they offered her a permanent position. She was regarded as a hardworking, intelligent, and handsome

HATTAR

FÖR

DAMER

OCH

FLICKOR

"EDIT"
Damhatt i tagal-
fläta. Finnes i vitt,
svart, marin, grå-
blått, beige, grönt,
rött och grått.
Kr. 11.50

"VANJA"
Damhatt i manilla-
fläta. Finn. i svart,
marin, brunt, grå-
blått, rost, grönt,
vitt
Kr. 9.75

"MARGIT"
Damhatt i liséré-
fläta. Finnes i
marin o. beige
brunt o. beige
rosa o. beige
grönt o. beige
rost o. beige

Kr. 7.25

"VERA"
Damhatt i tagalfl., band-
kantad. Finnes i svart,
marin, brunt, beige, rost,
gråblått, grönt, lila, rött,
vitt .... Kr. 18.—

"OLGA"
Damhatt i eng. skinn.
Storlek 57—61 cm.
Kr. 4.75

Greta Gustafsson in PUB mail order catalog

employee; no one on the staff at Bergström's seems to have realized that they were dealing with a headstrong young woman who was determined upon a career on the stage or in films. She was interested in her work and amused by it, but once she was outside the store, all her thoughts were concentrated on acting and she talked of nothing else.

Early in 1921, when Bergström's was preparing its spring mail-order catalog with a print order of fifty thousand copies to be sent all over Sweden, she was given the task of modeling hats. Originally it was decided to employ a professional actress, but when the advertising manager saw her, put a hat on her head, and studied the effect, he concluded that he already possessed an excellent model and need go no farther. So it happened that in the spring catalog, on page 109, Greta Lovisa Gustafsson is shown modeling five hats ranging in price from 4.75 to 18 kronor. The hats were given names: Edit, Vanja, Margit, Vera, and Olga. In this improbable manner she appeared before the Swedish public for the first time.

Later, for the summer mail-order catalog, she modeled five more hats, which were rather more expensive, ranging in price from 10 to 26 kronor and bearing the names Clary, Ethel, Jane, Helny, and Solveig. In the interval she had become more mature. In the spring photographs she might be taken for eighteen or nineteen, but in the summer photographs she might be taken for a serious young matron, very much in command of herself, aged about twenty-five. In fact she was only fifteen.

Her friends in the studios were still looking out for parts for her. In the spring of 1921, about the time that she was being photographed modeling the summer hats, she was given her first small role in a film. She asked for and received a week's leave of absence and then joined the cast of a film being made by John W. Brunius, the 35-year-old director of the Skandia Film Company. Only her most intimate friends knew what she was doing, and they were sworn to secrecy.

Brunius was then making a series of historical films remarkable for their cleverness and quiet charm. He was not a great filmmaker. He had none of Sjöström's marvelous sense of composition or Stiller's genius for bringing a heightened sense of drama to everything he touched. He wanted to tell the story of Sweden's past with gentleness and gaiety, and had already completed a number of films of this kind. He was now engaged in casting for a film called *En Lyckoriddare* (*The Gay Cavalier*), based on a story by Harald Molander, a brother of the director of the Royal Dramatic Academy. He interviewed Greta Lovisa, was delighted with her charm and eagerness, and gave her the role of a maidservant in a tavern scene. It was a bit part, for there were many maidservants and the gay cavalier, played with great verve by Gösta Ekman,

Our Daily Bread, *1921*

frolicked with them all. The feminine lead was given to Mary Johnson, the young actress who had acted so magnificently in Stiller's *Sir Arne's Treasure*. In this costume drama Greta Lovisa's face appears for a little less than two minutes.

Her name did not appear in the credits, and no one paid very much attention to the young actress, who might have been in serious trouble if Bergström's learned that she was moonlighting. Meanwhile the advertising manager at Bergström's was showing an interest in short advertising films and seeking the advice of Captain Lasse Ring, a well-known maker of minor promotional films. He was a man who greatly enjoyed a joke, and he came up with the idea for a film to be called *How Not to Wear Clothes*. Olga Anderson, a professional actress, was hired to show how clothes should not be worn. Greta Lovisa quickly learned about the project, sought out Captain Ring, and was given a comedy role specially created for her. She appears in a well-tailored coat, high-buttoned boots, and a cloth cap with a visor—evidently a young woman about to be taken for a ride in an automobile. She is smiling and good-humored, rather coy. To her alarm her costume appears to disintegrate. A checkered skirt and a checkered scarf materialize out of nowhere, and with a certain amount of assistance provided by invisible lengths of elastic, her costume is transformed into a riding habit. The film lasted seven minutes, and only about two minutes were given to the actress who so desperately wanted to make films. Captain Ring noted that she performed a difficult role with aplomb, and decided to use her again as soon as possible. She took direction well, she possessed a genuine comic talent, and he thoroughly enjoyed working with her.

Later in the year, he made another advertising film with her in an even smaller part. Called *Our Daily Bread*, it promoted a local bakery. She is one of a number of girls seen eating very rich cakes in the roof garden of the Strand Hotel in Stockholm, and the humor of the film derives from the spectacle of young girls gorging themselves with chocolate cream buns and eclairs. A better title for the film might have been *How Not to Eat*. Greta Lovisa stuffs herself with cake in a manner suggesting that she has spent most of her life on a starvation diet, and when, from taking too big a bite, some of the cake slips out of her mouth, she stuffs it back again with a sudden display of energy worthy of a greater cause.

Within a year she had made three films. In each of them she had appeared only briefly, and all together she had been on screen for about ten minutes. Nevertheless she was now more than ever determined to become a film actress and could imagine no other life worth living. She knew that actors sometimes enter films by the purest chance, and she was waiting to pounce on the first opportunity.

The Coming of Garbo

One night in the summer of 1922 she was looking idly into the window of a bookshop when she became aware that a tall, wiry man with gray hair was gazing at her. She turned her face away, but he continued to gaze at her reflection in the glass, admiring her clear-cut profile, high cheekbones, and sculptured lips, and about that moment when he first caught sight of her, he said later, "I was like someone transfixed. She was astonishingly beautiful, like someone you see in a dream, and somehow I had the feeling that she was not Swedish at all. From that moment I was determined to use her."

Slightly annoyed by the stranger's attentions, Greta Lovisa slipped into the bookshop. He followed her. She picked up some books. He kept gazing at her. Then, becoming frightened, she rushed out of the store and ran most of the way home.

What happened afterward belongs almost to fantasy. By the purest accident the tall, wiry man came the next morning to the Ladies' Hats Department at Bergström's with two young actresses on his arms. His name was Erik Petschler, and he was a director of films that were not unlike Mack Sennett's slapstick comedies. Amusing, loud-voiced, with a gift for dialect and a pleasant streak of vulgarity, he demanded two elaborate hats for his two friends. There was a good deal of giggling and private horseplay before the hats were wrapped up and taken away. Greta Lovisa took no part in the sale, which was conducted by a senior saleslady, but she recognized the man who had followed her into the bookshop the previous evening. She asked who the man was, learned that he was Erik Petschler, looked up his name in the telephone directory, and called him up during the lunch break. He said he remembered her vividly and would be delighted to give her a screen test for a new comedy he hoped to produce shortly, to be called *Luffar-Petter* (*Peter the Tramp*). She did well in the test. It was now a simple matter of going to the floor manager at Bergström's and asking for a brief leave of absence while the film was being made. This might have been arranged quite easily if she had not made the mistake of saying she wanted the time off in order to act in a film. Bergström's disapproved of salesladies who showed too much interest in a film career, and she was told that she could certainly make the film on her own time, but the company had not the slightest intention of rearranging vacation schedules for her benefit. The unlucky interview was reported to Petschler, who cautioned her against leaving Bergström's without some assurance of financial security and the most he could pay her was ten kronor a day for the few days it would take to make the film. She spent a restless night and by morning had made her decision. Bergström's records include the brief notation: EMPLOYMENT ENDED: 22/7 1922, REASON FOR LEAVING: *To make films.*

Luffar-Petter, *Greta Gustafsson in center*

Luffar-Petter, *Greta Gustafsson leads procession*

Luffar-Petter is one of those plotless films that are made memorable precisely because they are plotless. No one, least of all Petschler, who directed it and played the two leading roles, knew what was going to happen next. He played the roles of a tramp called Petterson and a fire-brigade officer called Silverjälm; the tramp is a scoundrel and the fire-brigade officer is something of a dandy. The mayor of the local town has three daughters, played by Tyra Ryman, Irene Zetterberg, and Greta Gustafsson. To amuse themselves the three schoolgirls wear identical costumes, and when first we see them they are dressed in black shorts and black T-shirts and they are being drilled by the gymnastics mistress, who resembles a tree trunk and carries herself with portentous dignity. Such solemn dignity demands a pratfall, and the girls mischievously trip her up and give her a parting kick in the backside.

Fire-brigade officer Silverjälm is courting Greta and offers to take the three girls to Stockholm. During the journey they go bathing. The girls wear identical bathing suits and disport themselves in the water, on the shore, and around the pup tent they have put up for their own amusement. They catch a fish, and Greta promptly slaps Officer Silverjälm in the face with it. Enter the tramp, who observes that he possesses a considerable resemblance to the officer, steals his clothes, and hurries off to Stockholm. After the Mack Sennett bathing beauties comes the Mack Sennett chase, as the officer and the three girls go in pursuit of the tramp, whose long nose and wild hair make him easily recognizable. Finally the tramp is cornered, and the officer orders the fire hoses to be directed at him. When the tramp is last seen, he is being drenched by the fire hoses, and when the officer is last seen, he has abandoned his courtship of Greta and is being married to a rich widow.

The two-reel comedy has many defects, the most obvious being that everyone overacts. Greta overacts as much as anyone. Nevertheless the film is amusing, fast-paced, and original; if it attracted little attention it was because all Mack Sennett comedies look alike. The première took place at the Odeon Theatre in Stockholm on December 22, 1922. The Swedish magazine *Swing*, with tongue in cheek, announced the curious birth of a new Swedish star. Under her photograph were the words "Greta Gustafsson. May perhaps become a Swedish film star. Reason—her Anglo-Saxon appearance." The magazine was only a little bit more serious in its review of *Luffar-Petter*: "Although Miss Gustafsson has enjoyed the dubious pleasure of playing the role of a bathing beauty in Mr. Erik A. Petschler's fire department film, we have received no impression whatsoever of her capabilities. It is always a pleasure to record a new name in Swedish films, and we hope we shall have occasion to mention her again."

The Coming of Garbo

The truth is that she was not showing remarkable promise, and no one seeing the film could possibly have imagined that she had the makings of a great dramatic actress. What she needed above all was training and discipline. Petschler decided to introduce her to Frans Ewall, formerly the director of the Academy attached to the Royal Dramatic Theatre and then a private coach. Ewall had the reputation of a man with an instinctive understanding of young actresses. People said he could go through a crowd of girls and pick out those possessing dramatic talent simply by glancing at them. He interviewed Greta and liked her. Her teeth were bad, her hair was unkempt, she was gauche and nervous, but she had an excellent figure, walked gracefully, and was undeniably one of those who possess talent. But though he could recommend her for a scholarship at the Academy, he could do no more. The final test would come at the Royal Dramatic Theatre when she would stand alone on a bare stage before a committee of judges and act out her parts.

Every year in Stockholm there are two or three hundred applicants for these scholarships. The test is short, grueling, and deliberately arranged so that only the most dedicated students receive the award. The test takes place in a huge, drafty auditorium. The judges watch in silence. Not a flicker of an eyelid suggests their opinion of a performance. Only seven or eight students a year receive the grant, which enables them to study for three years in a few simple rooms, steeped in tradition, high above the Royal Dramatic Theatre.

The test took place in August 1922, shortly before her seventeenth birthday. She was sick with apprehension and did not sleep on the night before her appearance on the empty stage. With a crowd of other aspiring young actors and actresses she waited in a seemingly endless corridor for the time when she would be summoned to appear on the stage. The students were called alphabetically, and she was therefore luckier than most of them. She remembers going on the stage, but she could remember nothing that happened afterward except the agony of being closely watched, the horror of hearing her own echoing voice, and the consciousness that she was alone and that her whole future depended upon her performances in three short extracts from three plays. These had been chosen for her by Frans Ewall. She played an excerpt from Victorien Sardou's *Madame Sans-Gêne*. As Catherine Hubscher, the former laundry woman who married a sergeant in Napoleon's army who later became a Marshal of France, she trounced everyone in sight in a wonderfully fierce explosion of gutter language. She also played excerpts from a play by Selma Lagerlöf and from Ibsen's *Lady from the Sea*. She did well in all of them, and three days later she received the news that she had been accepted. She said later, "I was so excited, I thought I would die of joy."

Luffar-Petter

The Royal Dramatic Academy in Stockholm is one of the most difficult acting schools in the world. The drama students are trained like athletes. They must live only for acting. Taught to develop their personalities, encouraged to work with each other in couples, not in groups, they are required to assume their own distinctive styles and at the same time to follow a regimen that destroys all extravagance of temperament. For the first year she was still on trial. In the second year, after an exhausting examination, she would become a contract pupil receiving about forty dollars a month. Students were expected to live like monks and nuns in holy dedication to their art, and were watched closely for idiosyncrasies. They had a crowded schedule, with hardly a moment for themselves. A normal day would start at eight in the morning with an hour of dramatic acting followed by an hour of classical study, an hour of fencing, an hour of elocution. There were classes in diction, voice, posture, and make-up, which was studied with considerably more care than in most acting schools. In the evenings they put on plays or attended plays in the Royal Dramatic Theatre or elsewhere on free passes. From time to time they were given minor roles in regular performances. By the end of the three-year course half the students had dropped out.

Greta did well at the Academy, though she could have done much better. She was incorrigibly lazy, rebellious, and inattentive at her lessons. She did whatever she pleased and was careless of the consequences. Worse still, she set an example for the others, who also became lazy, rebellious, and inattentive. Her saving grace was that she was so obviously talented and so obviously kindhearted that what in another student would be regarded as rudeness and indifference was taken for exuberance and shyness. When she acted, she threw her whole life into it, and when she was not acting, she was frivolous or spent long hours in moody silence.

Maria Schildknecht, who taught dramatics, said many years later: "She was much more beautiful then than she is now. She always gave a beautifully clean performance, but suffered from a kind of indolence." Karl Nygren, one of the directors of the Theatre, remembered that she had a fine contralto voice with a nice depth and resonance. The students performed many plays for themselves. Greta performed in a production of Arthur Schnitzler's *Farewell Supper*, taking the part of a whore, which she played excellently, but she could play the part of a sophisticated woman just as easily. She played a lady's maid in J. M. Barrie's *The Admirable Crichton*, but she was remembered most for her playing of Hermione in *The Winter's Tale*:

The Emperor of Russia was my Father;
Oh that he were alive, and here beholding
His daughter's trial; that he did but see
The flatness of my misery; yet with eyes
Of pity, not revenge!

She is known to have played in a German comedy, *The Tortoise Shell*; in a Russian drama, *Violins of Autumn*; and in Jules Romains' intellectual farce *Knock, or The Triumph of Medicine*. In the brief time she spent at the Academy she was obviously kept very busy.

She played boys' parts with wonderful success, moving and laughing like a boy, but she was best in romantic tragedies. She could assume the Valkyrie look with ease, but she could also play raw comedy with exquisite timing. What endeared her to her long-suffering teachers was the extraordinary range of her abilities. They felt she could act any part once she set her mind to it.

In her quiet, boisterous way she was happy at the Academy, though too eccentric to become popular. She made few friends. Her closest companion was Mona Martenson, who was also a madcap. Mimi Pollak was another friend; small-boned, with a narrow, eager face, she was one of those who are destined to spend their whole lives on the stage. These three young actresses formed a kind of conspiratorial society with the avowed object of protecting each other and defying the laws of the Royal Dramatic Academy. They were enjoying their newfound independence.

The circumstances of life at the Academy almost demanded very close friendships between actresses; they were narcissistic and at the same time in love with one another. High-strung, beautiful, and ambitious, they instinctively behaved like young aristocrats while they were studying at the Academy, living in a world totally removed from the real world, and every night they returned to their plebeian apartment houses, and Greta's was the most plebeian of all. Another student, Holger Löwenadler, remembered being especially struck by two things about her: the beauty of her voice and how she was always saying with an air of astonishment, "It isn't possible! To think I have come from Blekingegatan!" He said nothing about her physical beauty, and in fact no one at the Academy regarded her as strikingly beautiful.

One day in the spring of 1923, Gustaf Molander, the director-in-chief of the Academy, received a message from Mauritz Stiller, inquiring about the progress of the young student Greta Gufstafsson. Stiller had been hearing good reports of her, and he was beginning to work on a new film in which there might be a suitable part for her. Molander was

Mauritz Stiller

evasive. He thought she needed considerably more training and experience; she had spent only a few months at the Academy; it was too early to think of her acting professionally. Stiller was insistent. Finally, Molander agreed to send her to Stiller's house for an interview.

When Greta arrived at the house there was no sign of Stiller. She sat down on a chair in the great shadowy hall and waited interminably. Two hours passed. There was still no sign of him. When he arrived at last, accompanied by a huge wolfhound, she was trembling and almost out of her mind.

Stiller had a curious habit of looking at people as though he were looking through them or beyond them. He seemed not to see them, but in fact he was continually watching and appraising them. His manner was strange and distant. He asked a few routine questions: her age, what experience she had had besides her work at the Academy, and he nodded when she answered. Actually he was examining her closely and deliberately exercising the director's privilege of submitting his actors to shock treatment. Afterward he remembered every detail of her clothes, her manner, the way she answered his questions. Suddenly he was saying casually, "Well, why don't you take off your hat and coat?" Greta burst out laughing. There had been long silences intermingled with casual questions, and this last question made no sense to her. She fumbled with the coat, and suddenly he turned away and said, as though speaking to the wall, "What's your telephone number?" It sounded like the usual question asked by a director before dismissing an applicant. Nervously she looked up at him, but he seemed to be lost in thought. As she slipped away, she heard him muttering, "I will remember you." But she had the feeling that he had completely forgotten her already.

A few weeks later, when work on the projected film based on Selma Lagerlöf's novel *Gösta Berlings Saga* had advanced a little farther, Stiller, still looking for an actress to play the role of Countess Elizabeth Dohna, telephoned the Royal Dramatic Academy and asked them to send over their two best actresses. He interviewed them, and was displeased with them. "They are excellent actresses," he said, "but they are not pretty enough." Someone reminded him of Mona Martenson and Greta Gustafsson, and he immediately drove to the theatre; he had a curious feeling that he must see them immediately, or all would be lost. He found Mona Martenson playing Jessica in *The Merchant of Venice*, but there was no sign of Greta Gustafsson, who had vanished on some mysterious errand of her own. He left a message, asking her to have lunch with him.

Once again, when Greta came to his house, there was no sign of Stiller. Instead she was greeted by the actor Axel Nilsson, who had been invited to the lunch and was just as puzzled as Greta by Stiller's absence. Once again Greta hovered in the hall, waiting. She refused to go into the dining room. She was shy, nervous, and confused. She was sure Stiller was playing some trick on her. Then quite suddenly, when she had given up all hope of seeing him, Stiller bounded into the house followed by the huge wolfhound. Axel Nilsson came out into the hall. Stiller shouted to him, "Well, she's come! What do you make of her, eh? Isn't she wonderful? My dear Miss Gustafsson, you are a little too fat, I believe. Axel, just look at those eyelashes! My dear lady, you'll have to lose twenty pounds if you are going to play the role I contemplate for you!" All the time he was turning her around and around like a top.

The script was being written by the young script writer Ragnar Hyltén-Cavallius, who had made his own inquiries about Greta Gustafsson and did not share Stiller's enthusiasm. He found her boring, without character, a healthy farm girl with a smattering of dramatic training. Stiller dismissed the charges categorically.

"You just don't understand her," he said. "She is shy and doesn't show what she feels, and she is really completely lacking in technique. But the important thing is that she is beautiful! Look at her feet—look at her heels! Have you ever seen such beautiful heels, such fine lines? And it is the same with her legs and her whole body!"

A few days later Greta Gustafsson and Mona Martenson were invited to take a screen test at the Råsunda film studios just outside Stockholm. Stiller hid behind a board, and through a hole watched the two actresses while he kept them waiting. When Greta heard about this trick later, she said, "He was watching me closely to see whether I had courage." She was in greater need of courage when the time came for the test, which was brief and relied largely on shock treatment. He kept them waiting for two hours, then ordered them to go directly to the make-up room, and it was another half hour before their faces were made up. Then they were introduced to the cameraman and the stagehands. The cameraman later remembered that Greta was entirely unassuming, curtsied to everyone on the lot, and trembled like a leaf. There was a sofa on the stage. At one point in the test Greta asked Stiller what she should do next. He roared at her, "Lie down and be sick!" He stood over her, threatening. "So you don't know how to be sick, eh? and you call yourself an actress!" he shouted. Greta lay on the sofa and gave a convincing impression of someone being violently ill. A moment later he barked, "That's enough! Now go home!"

Greta was beginning to understand Stiller. She was not terrified of him, and she had faith in herself: so much faith that the very next day she took the train to the studio to find out whether the test was successful. By coincidence she met Julius Jaenzon, Stiller's cameraman, on the train. She asked him shyly about the test, and he told her he was almost sure she had failed.

A few days later the telephone rang in her apartment; it was Stiller's voice saying she had performed magnificently in the test and would be given the role of Countess Elizabeth Dohna in *Gösta Berlings Saga.* Mona Martenson had also performed magnificently and would be given the role of Countess Ebba Dohna. Greta was delirious with joy. Some weeks passed before the contract was drawn up. Not until July 23, 1923, was she offered the final contract, by which Svensk Filmindustri agreed to pay her 3,000 kronor for her services, the equivalent of about $600. This was not a niggardly salary, for it corresponded to at least $3,000 in today's money. The contract was signed by Greta's mother, for Greta was still underage.

On November 9, 1923, another document was drawn up and signed by Anna Gustafsson in the presence of witnesses. This was a formal application to the Ministry of the Interior requesting permission for her daughter to adopt the legal name of Garbo. Less than a month later, on December 4, permission was granted. On that day Greta Lovisa Gustafsson died, and Greta Garbo was born.

The name, which became so memorable, was the invention of Mauritz Stiller, who had long cherished it and was determined to bestow it on an actress worthy of it. In his imagination the name suggested fairyland, romance, beauty, everything he had associated in his childhood with the utmost happiness and the wildest dreams. Many explanations were later offered to explain the name. Someone wrote that he derived it from the first letters of a sentence he wrote describing Greta Gustafsson: *Gör alla roller berömvärt opersonligt* (Plays all roles in a commendably impersonal fashion). Others remembered that *garbo* in Spanish and Italian is a rarely used word describing a peculiar kind of grace and charm. Still others imagined it was derived from the name of Erica Darbo, a famous Norwegian singer of the time. A more plausible explanation can be found in the *garbon*, a mysterious sprite that sometimes comes out at night to dance to the moonbeams. This elfin creature was a descendant of the dreaded *gabilun* of Swedish and German folklore, who was killed by Kudrun. The *gabilun* breathed fire from its nostrils and could assume any shape at will, and some memory of his ancient power remained in the *garbon*, just as Robin Goodfellow retains some features of the Great God Pan. No one knows the true origin of the word. When asked about it, Stiller simply looked up in the air, smiled, and said, "I really don't know. But it's right, isn't it?"

The name found a home with the daughter of Carl Alfrid Gustafsson, and the reign of the mysterious Greta Garbo had begun.

The Young Countess

I'm very sorry. You'll just have to
burn a little longer.
                    —Mauritz Stiller

I<small>N THE HISTORY</small> of Greta Garbo, two films, now rarely seen, occupy
a special place. These are *Gösta Berlings Saga*, directed by Stiller, and
Die Freudlose Gasse (The Street of Sorrows), directed by Georg
Wilhelm Pabst. In these films for the first time the mysterious mask
Greta Garbo presented to the screen was tentatively explored, examined
in various lights, interpreted, refined, thrown into shadow—a mask of
astonishing beauty and effortless intelligence. It was as though at long
last the film had found its ideal creation. Her face opened up like a
flower, very pale, with a terrible fragility about it and a strange nobility,
as though she had descended from an ancient race that had nearly perished from the earth; and indeed, with that trace of Lapp blood she
inherited from her mother, she was in fact descended from one of the
most ancient and mysterious of all races. No one who set eyes on that
face ever forgot it. There was something in it of the goddess, and of the
undeveloped girl, and of a woman at a moment of quiet and intense passion. Time, action, argument—all were suspended when you watched
that face. Stiller had chosen well. During the many months of filming
Gösta Berlings Saga, he was continually marveling at her strange beauty.
He was in love with her, but he was also a director attempting to see her

coldbloodedly, determined to extract the maximum of art from her performance.

"You don't understand," he would say, whenever anyone objected to her uneven performance. "There is something quite extraordinary about her. She is as nervous as a fish, and she can't think. I don't believe a real thought has ever entered her head. I have to break her down. I am merciless with her. But when she is broken down, what a performance she gives—such calm, such concentration, such effortless knowledge. And besides all this, her face, which is not really so terribly beautiful, though of course she would be worth staring at in the street, becomes when she is acting a face to make the gods happy."

Stiller was wildly excited by his discovery and took endless trouble with her. There were woods just outside the Råsunda studios, and the actors grew accustomed to seeing Garbo and Stiller walking slowly together at the edge of the woods, Stiller gesticulating, Garbo silent, pale, simply listening and absorbing everything the director told her. He dominated her completely. On the set he spoke to her rarely, communicating by gesture. He was like a magician, conjuring out of her tall, graceful, athletic body and sensitive face a refinement that had never existed before. The girl from Blekingegaten was becoming a countess, the descendant of a long aristocratic line. Sometimes during the long painful process that Stiller called "breaking her down," there were moments of rebellion. At such moments Garbo's face was transformed, and a surprised camera crew would see her shuddering, her face flushed and contorted, her eyes filling with tears, as she muttered, "I hate you, Stiller! I hate you! I hate you!" Then Stiller would smile. Those terrible moments told him that he was succeeding in destroying the last vestiges of the daughter of Karl Alfrid Gustafsson. In her place there would emerge a supreme artist of the screen.

Although Stiller was playing the role of Svengali, he was playing it with kindness and affection. He had always wanted to mold and shape an actress into greatness. He had hoped to do this with Mary Johnson, who played Elsalill in *Sir Arne's Treasure*, but felt he had failed. With Garbo, still young and unspoiled, he felt he was succeeding.

Garbo said afterward she enjoyed making the film, but it was like passing through a terrible fire. Stiller was teaching her to act with her whole being, but she was not yet strong enough for that complete absorption in a role. There were days when she felt she had no existence except as the Countess Elizabeth Dohna, and other days when she recognized herself only too well. Then she would sit in a corner and try to summon out of the air, out of memory, out of the things Stiller had told her, the magic word that would transform her once more into the heroic

young countess who lived shortly after the Napoleonic wars. At night she went home exhausted. "I could not weep anymore," she said. "I was wrung dry."

A reluctant Garbo was interviewed on the set by a journalist, Inga Gaate.

"Please don't sit there and write down everything that slips out of my mouth," Garbo said. "I am one of those people who don't think—I talk first and think later."

"Well, tell me, is it very hard to make movies?"

"Terribly hard! It has been a Gethsemane! Stiller is the most generous person in the world; he never gets angry; he is never melancholy, however much he scolds me. He shapes people according to his will. As for me, I am one of those nice, ordinary people who suffer terribly if someone is mean to them. In this life women should have a little forwardness, even if it is not very womanly—and that wonderful forwardness is something I have very little of."

That "wonderful forwardness" was indeed something she would lack all her life, but she was far from being a nice, ordinary person. She was complex, willful, difficult, and demanding, and she was all the more demanding because Stiller had trained her to demand the utmost from herself.

Gösta Berlings Saga is many stories, some created by Stiller and Ragnar Hylten-Cavallius, who wrote the script, others taken from the pages of Selma Lagerlöf's book, and still others improvised during the months of filming. It is a director's film, every inch of it being permeated with Stiller's sense of space and movement, his feeling for beauty, his instinct for drama. He seems to have guessed it would be the last good film he would ever be allowed to make. After this there would be only a succession of failures.

The original story, as written by Selma Lagerlöf, describes a favorite period of Swedish novelists. The Napoleonic wars had ended, and all over Sweden there were former officers at loose ends, with incomes too small to support them. They spent their lives visiting friends, carousing, wenching, creating trouble. Sometimes, when they stayed in the houses of their rich friends, they put on entertainments that were regarded as a form of payment for benefits bestowed on them. Thus one whole wing of Ekeby Castle is filled with these lively former officers, and the mistress of the castle feeds and indulges them, and joins in their dances, theatricals, and sleighing parties. She is immensely wealthy from the neighboring iron mines and can well afford to keep these pensioners. A middle-aged woman, she is estranged from her mother, who once uttered a curse on her and on Ekeby Castle.

The Young Countess

Nearby, at Borg, in the house of Count Henrik Dohna, the young Countess Elizabeth is growing to maturity. A tutor is found for her. The handsome young tutor with the flashing eyes is Gösta Berling, an unfrocked priest thrown out of his own church by his parishioners, who were infuriated by his fiery sermons, loose living, and drunkenness. The young Countess falls in love with him, but inevitably his past is discovered, and he is dismissed from the household. He goes to Ekeby Castle to live with the pensioners and spend his days carousing, still dreaming of his hopeless love for the young Countess. When he meets Marianne Sinclair, who is also beautiful, he is torn between his two loves. "I am Gösta Berling, the lord of ten thousand kisses and thirteen thousand love letters," he says, but it is not true. Like all romantic heroes he is searching for one abiding love and cannot find her. He rants and makes wild gestures, suffers terribly, calls upon heaven to witness his suffering, and is happy nowhere.

Meanwhile at Ekeby Castle a certain Captain Kristian Bergh is up to savage mischief. He has become the ruler of the pensioners, the power in Ekeby Castle. He hounds the mistress of Ekeby out of her castle, reminding her of the curse laid on her by her mother, and then turns on Marianne Sinclair, accusing her of being a woman of easy virtue. In the dead of winter Marianne flees across the snow. When Gösta Berling learns of her flight, he immediately harnesses his sleigh and goes after her, finding her at last in the snowdrifts, half-dead. He returns with her to the castle, and soon the mistress of Ekeby returns, having made her peace with her mother. Hating the hard-drinking cavaliers, she calls upon the local villagers to burn down the wing of the castle where they live. In the depths of night, when the cavaliers have feasted and fallen asleep, the villagers set fire to the building. Marianne and Gösta Berling are trapped inside, and from far away the young Countess Elizabeth, attending a ball in honor of her approaching marriage, sees the flames of Ekeby. She is still hopelessly in love with her former tutor, and while Gösta Berling is frantically trying to rescue Marianne, the young Countess runs across the snow to the castle. Marianne is rescued, and Gösta Berling is about to wander away, having no more desire to stay at Ekeby, when he sees the Countess. He offers to drive her back to Borg. She accepts. They are sitting in the sleigh and talking about their past lives when they are attacked by wolves, but they escape from them. Gösta Berling swears he will rebuild Ekeby and live like a real man. Finally he marries the Countess, and the mistress of Ekeby gives them her castle and the villagers proclaim their affection for the newly married couple.

Such, briefly, is the story that Stiller and Ragnar Hylten-Cavallius

Lars Hanson

extracted from the long and richly poetic novel, which no one had previously dared to put on film because the story was so intricately woven out of countless characters and subplots that it was almost impossible to conceive of it in film terms. In the end Stiller's film ran for four hours, but even so he had ridden roughshod over a vast tapestry. He compressed and sometimes omitted important incidents in the story. At other times he expanded relentlessly, using the story as a background for his own improvisations. Greta Garbo in the character of the young Countess was the most astonishing of all those improvisations.

Her love scenes are wonderfully luminous, and every emotion registers on her face. Lars Hanson, playing Gösta Berling, overacted and became a caricature of the romantic hero, but it scarcely matters, for when they were together one saw only Garbo. Already she was displaying her strange power to dominate the screen, so that everyone around her seemed to dissolve. Her acting was uneven. She was not always in command of herself. There were moments when, although she was on the screen, she seemed to be completely lost and withdrawn, as though she had not the least idea what she was doing, as though she was sleepwalking, and at such times her face was expressionless and even commonplace. This, too, sometimes happened in the films she made later. But at her best she casts a radiance around her. The love scenes, her appearance at the ball, her walk across the snow toward Ekeby Castle, the sudden look of frozen horror on her face when Gösta Berling was dismissed from the house, her expression during the sleigh ride with the wolves howling around her—all these were accomplished with a memorable delicacy at white heat. As she walks through a deserted house holding a candle on a level with her eyes, or dances in a ballroom in an empire dress, or simply gazes across the snow at the burning castle, she is vividly alive, and she has only to move through a garden picking flowers in a mood of dreamy abstraction for the viewer to feel that he is in the presence of something very close to divinity. Beauty itself became drama.

Stiller's passion for her was being subtly transmuted into film; he was bathing her in the light of his own exalted imagination. She moves through the story like a cool and godlike presence, and at the same time she is able to suggest a young woman in the torments of love. There are times when her face seems almost transparent and ghostlike, with the dewy coldness of the dead, and then Stiller will suddenly conjure from her so much warming life that we are no longer aware of the story—only of the radiance of her smile flowing from the screen. She seemed to know things no woman had ever dared to say. When her lips moved, she seemed to be speaking gravely and trustingly about matters we have only guessed at. Who she is, what she is doing in the story, become irrel-

evant; she is immune from the temptations of the storyteller. Like Helen
of Troy she moves through the story and is the prime cause of all that
happens, and yet is remote from it. We are not concerned with what
happens to her, because we know that nothing bad or good can ever
happen to her, for perfect beauty is unassailable. If she died, we would
not believe it. If she fell in love, that too would be very nearly incredi-
ble.

The drama lies elsewhere: in the sense of expectation aroused by her
presence. She knows all the secrets of the earth, and if we wait a little
while, she will declare them to us. She never declares them, but they are
suggested by her gestures, her smile, her eyes. The promise remains a
promise, never to be fulfilled in the story, but fulfilled in the mysterious
communication between herself and the audience. She is closer to the
audience than to the other characters on the screen. She speaks to the
audience directly, even though she remains silent. When she sits at night
beside the candle on her dressing table, she is a woman brooding over all
the mysteries that women brood over at night, and she is able to convey
this sense of brooding mystery and quietness.

Lars Hanson gave a bravura performance but was so rarely credible
that it would have made little difference if he had simply been painted
on a backdrop. Gerda Lundeqvist was completely convincing as the mistress of Ekeby, who lived under her mother's curse. With her lined face
and large haunted eyes, her ravaged beauty, her vigor and decisiveness,
she presents herself as the true aristocrat, and we believe she is quite capable of filling a wing of her castle with a crowd of pensioners and caring
deeply for them. She moves as though she owns the neighborhood, as
indeed she does, for she is the sole owner of nine iron mines. Above all,
Gerda Lundeqvist was a dramatic actress of extraordinary talent. The
most memorable single scene in the film takes place when the mistress of
Ekeby finally meets her mother and the curse is lifted from her as they
silently yoke themselves to the mill and turn it like laboring beasts. It is a
short scene played with brutal simplicity and elemental strength; the
wheel becomes the wheel of destiny, and the two women, one of them
old and bent, the other in middle age, become elemental beings of an
ancient mythological drama, and all this is done so subtly that we are not
immediately aware that we are in the presence of mythologies. The old
woman is a shriveled crone, witchlike, while the mistress of Ekeby possesses a wonderful humanity.

Selma Lagerlöf described Count Henrik Dohna as "an ugly, stupid
man, who never turned his head without his whole body following it."
The role was played by Torsten Hammarén, one of the great clowns of
the Swedish Little Theatre, with icy distinction but without feeling,

with the result that his acting lacks conviction. Baroness Ellen Hartman-Cederström played the Countess Martha Dohna and acted with a vivid sense of her own nobility; she belonged entirely to those vast rococo interiors. The only bad performance was given by Mona Martenson, who was miscast as Elizabeth's sister.

Stiller was well served by his art director, Vilhelm Bryde, a well-known architect and art dealer who designed the sets and costumes. Stiller insisted that everything, or nearly everything, had to be authentic, and Bryde traveled up and down the country in search of period furniture. Stiller joined in the search, taking Garbo with him, teaching her the elements of style, encouraging her to learn everything that could be known about furniture. His teaching bore fruit: she developed a taste for rococo and still haunts antique shops.

Forty-eight separate sets were built at the Rasunda studios. Stiller pored over the hundreds of designs submitted to him by Vilhelm Bryde and by Ingrid Gunther, a young costume designer. He called on museum directors, connoisseurs, and antique dealers for advice and help. Antique shops were ransacked for exactly the right paneling, writing tables, chandeliers, doors, and windows. Floors were ripped out of old houses and laid down in the studios. An old fireplace, discovered in northern Sweden, was brought to Stockholm. And Stiller hinted darkly that it would be necessary to have authentic wolves in the scene of the sleigh ride. Then he relented and suggested that police dogs might do just as well. Karl Svensson, a friendly industrialist whom Garbo had known when she was a lather girl, lent them his wolfhound. More wolfhounds were borrowed from the Stockholm police. The dogs' tails were weighted with lead to prevent them from wagging. The scene was filmed at Hammarby on an icy waste during the middle of winter. Men with guns stood around to keep any real wolves at bay, while the police dogs hurled themselves at the sleigh.

Stiller's passion for authenticity extended to the huge set in the Rasunda studios representing Ekeby Castle. He was determined to burn down the wing of the building where the pensioners lived. To ensure a magnificent conflagration he ordered strips of celluloid glued to the walls and drenched the floors with gasoline. He enjoyed himself greatly —a sandwich in one hand, a megaphone in the other. "There he was, roaring like a lion, sweat pouring down his face, enjoying himself like a boy who runs off and jumps on a fire engine to watch his first fire," wrote a newspaper reporter. He could be seen clambering up the ladders where the cameramen were leaning close to the flames. Then he would drop down and bellow at a cameraman to take a shot from the ground at an angle he wanted. At one moment Lars Hanson was hanging perilously close to the burning roof beams.

Gerda Lundeqvist and Greta Garbo

"It's all right!" Stiller shouted. "Don't be cautious! Keep going! If the flames come closer, that's all right—it won't look like a real fire unless you show some courage!"

"You're shouting so loud you'll blow me off the roof!" Hanson shouted back.

A few minutes later Stiller observed that there were real firemen on the set and they were pouring water on the burning building.

"What the devil are you doing with that water?" he roared at them. "Who thought of bringing up the hoses? It's absolutely monstrous!"

He was told that the hoses were being tested against an emergency. He seemed satisfied, but allowed no more water to fall on his beloved flames.

He was like a man in a trance, enchanted by flames. He was completely fearless. There was a moment when the horses in the pensioners' wing of the castle seemed about to stampede. He just laughed. Once when Hanson was crawling beside a burning wall, Stiller decided that the camera angle he had previously decided upon must be changed. There were delays while he tried to work out a better camera angle. The flames were licking Hanson's knees.

"I'm burning!" Hanson screamed.

"I'm very sorry," Stiller answered. "You'll just have to burn a little longer."

When Stiller was asked later whether he had enjoyed making the film, he laughed and said, "You ask me that, and we burned Ekeby Castle and photographed Greta Garbo!" It was as though he found equal pleasure in the roaring flames and in the fragile, delicate beauty of his protégée.

While making the film, they had been drawn closer together than either had thought possible. Stiller, a homosexual, was becoming more and more enthralled by Garbo's beauty and innocence, and was continually in her company. Hjalmar Lenning, a friend of Stiller's and the foremost theatre critic of his time, was puzzled by the relationship. Garbo was, in his view, so terribly boring and quiet, that it was inexplicable that Stiller should be interested in her. "What do you see in her?" Lenning asked, and Stiller answered, "I have taught her everything; she takes instruction carefully; she is like wax in my hands." He spoke of her beauty, her immense potentiality, and the future opening up for her. But Swedish girls are rarely wax in the hands of older men, and it is far more likely that he was wax in her hands.

When the shooting was finished, Stiller was the first to complain about the quality of his own work on the film. The direction was uneven—brilliant passages followed by indifferent work that could have been done by almost any other director. The brilliance of occasional scenes

knit together the whole; the flames leaped up but there were long periods when they vanished among the embers. There were technical faults he could have avoided if there had been more time and more money at his disposal. He complained about the lighting in some scenes, but it was too late to reshoot them, and too much of the film was in medium shot. Throughout the film, except when Garbo or Gerda Lundeqvist appeared, there was a disturbing sense of strain. There was a sense in which he had been telling his own story, using Selma Lagerlöf's novel as a scaffolding. Neither the burning of the castle nor the scene in which Gösta Berling and the Countess flee across the snow was important in the novel, yet he had attached quite extraordinary importance to them. Why? He did not know, and no one dared to suggest to him that the burning castle might be himself, the gifted director burning himself out long before he has been given a chance to display the full measure of his gifts, while the wild sleigh ride perhaps reflects his own pursuit of Garbo.

When she finished playing in the film, Garbo returned to the Royal Dramatic Academy. Molander, encouraged by Stiller, offered her a contract as a "leading pupil," which meant an increase of salary and the privilege of acting on the stage of the Royal Dramatic Theatre. But she was in a restless mood, often failed to attend her lessons, liked to sit up talking through the night, and was something of a nuisance to her teachers.

On March 10, 1924, *Gösta Berlings Saga: Part I* opened at the Röda Kvarn (Red Barn) Theatre in Stockholm. The second part opened a week later. The film is inordinately long, amounting to fourteen reels, and while the critics approved of the film and paid special attention to Garbo and Gerda Lundeqvist, there were some who wondered why Selma Lagerlöf's novel had been treated so cavalierly. Everyone knew the novel and had fixed ideas about the characters in it. Then why had Stiller taken it upon himself to rewrite it? He was accused of being lighthearted in his approach to the Swedish classics, but forgiven because he had made a spectacular success out of intractable material.

Gösta Berlings Saga was bought by the Trianon Company in Germany and had its premiere in Berlin at the Mozart Theatre on the Nollendorffplatz. The Trianon Company paid 100,000 marks for the right to show the film—an unheard of amount in those days. Garbo accompanied Stiller to the premiere, receiving an ovation. She said a few well-chosen words in German and then vanished into the obscurity of her hotel.

While in Berlin, Stiller was asked why he had chosen an inexperienced actress to play the role of Countess Elizabeth Dohna. He answered simply that he wished all parts were played by inexperienced actors. He said, "I venture the paradox that films, as well as stage productions, ought to be played by amateurs, if they can only do it. When an actor is really 'great,' he is always trying to simplify his means of expression. He is always trying to get back to the natural simplicity that was his when he knew nothing about the technique of acting. This is the most difficult thing of all."

This theory, which has never commended itself to teachers of acting, would seem to be unanswerable.

Soon Stiller and his protégée returned to Stockholm to make plans for the next film. The memoirs of a White Russian refugee, Vladimir Semitioff, were appearing in the Sunday supplements of the newspaper *Stockholms-Tidningen*, and one of the stories recounted by Semitioff caught Stiller's eye. Called "The Odalisque from Smolny," it describes the adventures of an aristocratic young Russian woman who escaped from the Smolny Convent in Petrograd, where Lenin had his headquarters during the Russian Revolution. She made her way to Constantinople, fell in with some rascally Turks, was forced to join a harem, suffered a fate worse than death, and was finally rescued. The story, as Semitioff wrote it, was largely concerned with the young woman's escape from Russia, but Stiller was more interested in the exotic events that happened in Constantinople. He met Semitioff, bought the rights for the story, and spent the summer working on the script in his house on Bosön Island, near Stockholm. From time to time Semitioff came to visit him, and there were long discussions with Ragnar Hylten-Cavallius, the script writer, but most of the script appears to have been written by Stiller. By the middle of August the script was finished. The major roles were to be played by Garbo, who was to be the odalisque from Smolny, and by Einar Hanson, who, if he grew a beard, could be taken for the Turkish owner of the harem. Stiller delighted in crowd scenes, and he planned a spectacular scene with thousands of Turks rushing into the sea.

The Trianon Company, pleased with the success of *Gösta Berlings Saga*, was prepared to offer Stiller almost anything he wanted. But when they read the script, they were horrified. They begged Stiller to make a film with more box-office appeal, and suggested he should adapt a current novel dealing with life in a grand hotel. He refused. At all costs he was determined to make *The Odalisque from Smolny*. It had become an obsession. He dictated his terms. He wanted 150,000 marks for directing the film, while Garbo and Hanson were each to receive 500 marks a month and a five-year contract from Trianon. In the midst of prolonged negotiations he took to his bed. His health was restored when Trianon finally agreed to his conditions. Stiller made one compromise. He had insisted on taking his own cameraman, Julius Jaenzon, and a Swedish camera crew, while Trianon had insisted that he should take a German cameraman and a German camera crew. In the end he took Jaenzon and two German assistants. When all the contracts were signed, he took off for Turkey with Garbo, Einar Hanson, Jaenzon, Hylten-Cavallius, and the two Germans. As usual Stiller lived in grand style, spending money prodigally. He set up his headquarters at the Pera Palace Hotel, conducted himself like a potentate visiting one of his more remote colonies, and was accompanied by his cameramen whenever he left the hotel on those tours of inspection that were described as "gathering up atmosphere." He took to wearing a fez, talked gibberish and pretended it was Turkish, invented fantastic Turkish menus, explored the bazaars, bought carpets for his new house on Bosön Island, and enjoyed himself as he had never enjoyed himself before.

Stiller in Constantinople was not altogether a pleasant sight, for he was becoming recklessly self-indulgent. As a child he had lived in great poverty; his mother committed suicide when he was three years old; his father, a musician in the Russian Army, died a few years later. Adopted by a Jewish cap-maker in Helsinki, he spent a miserable youth before drifting into the theatre. To avoid service in the Russian Army he slipped out of Finland and joined the Little Theatre in Stockholm, first as an actor, then as a director and manager. From being a stage director he became a director of low-budget films. Tall and immaculate, with a prominent nose, large head, large hands and feet, he carried himself with the air of a man with no cares in the world. In fact he was deeply troubled, riddled with self-doubt, and at the mercy of his demons. He worked prodigiously hard, but was nearly always in debt. He had become a legend and had difficulty living up to it. Now, in Constantinople, he succumbed to all the vices of luxury and ostentation. It was as though the shackles had been removed from him and he was free at last to indulge all his fantasies.

Einar Hanson discovered that growing a beard was not an unalloyed pleasure. He refused to show himself, became moody, and against Stiller's advice resumed his dangerous passion for fast cars. He was likely to be arrested when he returned to Sweden for his part in an automobile accident. In Constantinople there was another accident, but Hanson emerged unscathed. Garbo went on long, lonely walks, exploring Constantinople to her heart's content. At a party given in the Pera Palace Hotel, she danced with Hylten-Cavallius, wearing a Chinese costume of brick-red silk embroidered with gold flowers. They danced the *hambo*, a very fast Swedish dance, and everyone applauded.

But there was very little reason to rejoice. Stiller was spending money on so vast a scale that they were bankrupt by the beginning of the year. He was able to borrow more money from a friendly Russian. He telegraphed to the Trianon Company in Berlin, asking in his lordly fashion for a million marks to be sent immediately to his account in Constantinople. There was no reply. He took the train to Berlin only to discover that the Trianon Company had failed and government investigators were examining the company's books. Garbo and Hanson were stranded in Constantinople with no money to pay for their railroad tickets to Berlin. Their tickets were eventually paid for by the Swedish Embassy. *The Odalisque from Smolny* was a disaster.

Even in poverty Stiller continued to live in the grand manner, piling up debts. Garbo and Hanson joined him at the Esplanade Hotel, which was among the best in Berlin. The directors of the Trianon Company had been jailed; Stiller was desperate but full of plans; he would go to Hollywood; he would preside over a great consortium of studios and cinemas embracing all of Europe; his star was rising; he could not fail. While he was discussing his projects with financiers, he was having the greatest difficulty paying for his food at the hotel.

Early in the spring, Georg Wilhelm Pabst, a German director who had produced two short films, was searching for a young actress to play the daughter of Councillor Rumfort in his film *Die Freudlose Gasse* (*The Street of Sorrows*), based on a story about the depression years in Vienna immediately after the war. Councillor Rumfort's daughter was to be young, frail, beautiful, and altogether appealing, the one luminous character in a film of otherwise unrelieved tragedy. To survive, and to keep her family alive, she would be forced to enter a house of prostitution, to entertain speculators and criminals, and to become involved in terrible intrigues. Pabst had seen and admired *Gösta Berlings Saga* and been impressed by Garbo's acting. But where to find her? She was rumored to be in Constantinople, in Stockholm, in Berlin. Finally she was found at the Esplanade Hotel, and there followed long and complex negotiations with Stiller for her services in the new film. Pabst was thirty-four years old, little known, small and ugly, badly dressed, and he was confronted by the famous and immaculate Stiller, who had been making films since 1912. Outwardly it must have appeared to be an unfair confrontation, but in fact all the advantages lay with Pabst, who had ample financial backing. Stiller, though penniless, drove a hard bargain. Pabst could have Garbo for a fee of $4,000 payable in American currency, but only on condition that Einar Hanson was given a part in the film and was paid the same fee, that Julius Jaenzon was employed as cameraman, and that only the very best Kodak film was used. Kodak film was then unavailable in Germany. Stiller agreed to a compromise by which Garbo's scenes would be photographed with Kodak film obtained from Paris but all other scenes would be photographed with the available Agfa film. Pabst insisted on having his own cameraman, and Stiller finally gave way. Shown the script, Stiller objected violently to some of the scenes written for Garbo and threatened to break off the negotiations unless changes were made. Some changes were made, and Stiller became an adviser on all matters concerning Garbo. He added a new scene, advised on the lighting, and gave lessons to Garbo on how she should play her part. There were many quarrels. Once Stiller said, "I am giving you Garbo so that you can make money, but I cannot let you ruin it!"

Pabst answered, "I'm not frightened. Perhaps I will die on the set. Perhaps I will have a heart attack. But I am not afraid of putting her in the picture, because I saw her in *Gösta Berlings Saga*. I'll manage it, and it is none of your business!"

It was very much Stiller's business, and he let no one forget it. To Garbo he said, "You have nothing to worry about. Pabst has seen *Gösta Berlings Saga* so many times that he knows everything about you. Half the year you will make films in Germany, and the other half you will make films in Sweden."

Garbo, elated by the new turn of events, entrusted herself all the more to Stiller's domination. He rehearsed her and directed her from a distance, advised her on costumes and make-up, and continued to play the role of Svengali. Garbo was his artistic possession on temporary loan to Pabst, who was well aware that she belonged to someone else. In *Gösta Berlings Saga* she played the role of the young Countess Elizabeth Dohna with exactly the right aristocratic ease. In *The Street of Sorrows* she played the starving young office worker, Greta Rumfort, who sells herself in order to survive, and she proved that she could play the part to perfection.

The Street of Sorrows

What need is there for romantic
treatment? Real life is too romantic
and too ghastly.
    —GEORG WILHELM PABST

GEORG WILHELM PABST was one of the giants of cinema, a man of
quite extraordinary ability. What distinguished him from other filmmakers was a strong sense of structure, a fierce intensity, and a deep sympathy for the suffering. He is remembered today for *Kamaradschaft*, *Die
Dreigroschenoper*, and *The White Hell of Pitz Palu*, all produced before
Hitler came to power. He remained in Germany under Hitler, but produced few films and none of any great distinction. Yet he left on his
films the imprint of a singularly intelligent mind with a wonderful gift
for looking unflinchingly into the dark places of the heart. He was one
of the very few intellectuals who have made films.

In appearance he resembled a theological student or a defrocked
priest. Thin, nervous, with piercing eyes, a hooked nose, and protruding
teeth, always wearing thick spectacles, he did not look like a man who
could take command of a studio. They said he might be taken for a jani-
tor or someone who had wandered in by mistake. But when he talked, he
was all fire and impatience, relentlessly determined to solve all problems
in the shortest time, forcing them to succumb to the power of his intelligence. In the cutting room, with the film hung snakelike around his

79

neck, a pair of scissors in his hand, busily squinting at the film and cutting it, he was an impressive figure, but he was more impressive on the set as he marched about, deep in thought, suddenly springing in one direction and then in another, adjusting a piece of furniture, tilting the head of an actor, deciding on the camera angles, ordering an actress to move a shade nearer the camera, and doing all these things simultaneously, or so it appeared. He was a tornado of activity just before he began shooting. Then when the camera was turning he would relapse once more into the mild-mannered theological student with the faint smile on his lips.

The Street of Sorrows was an adaptation of a novel by Hugo Bettauer that had been serialized in the Viennese newspaper *Neue Freie Presse*. Bettauer and Pabst were both Austrians, the setting of the novel was Vienna, and the characters were Viennese. The film, however, was being shot in Berlin, and the Viennese quality was subtly eroded. It was a harsh story of the rich and the poor in inflation-ridden Vienna immediately after World War I, and it became even harsher when set against a wintry Berlin background.

When Pabst met Stiller and acquired the services of Greta Garbo and Einar Hanson, he had already cast most of the characters. Werner Krauss was to play the butcher, Valeska Gert had the role of the procuress, the aging Asta Nielson was to play the prostitute who cold-bloodedly murders for her lover and just as cold-bloodedly sends him to the gallows, and Jaro Furth was given the role of the quiet, gentle government official who ruins himself by speculation. Greta Garbo was given the role of the official's daughter, and new incidents were added to the script so that Einar Hanson, who could look impressively American if necessary, could be cast as Lieutenant Davy, an American officer who falls in love with Garbo. Much of the rewriting appears to have been done hurriedly and Hanson, thrown into the film at the last minute, is never completely convincing.

For Greta Garbo the experience of playing the daughter of Councillor Rumfort was unnerving. Stiller had spent six months making *Gösta Berlings Saga*, working at a leisurely pace, paying careful attention to detail, and painting the lives of the aristocratic families of Borg and Ekeby on a wide canvas. Pabst was in a hurry. He wanted to complete a long and complicated film in a month. In fact, he completed it in thirty-four days by working his actors sixteen hours a day. Unlike Stiller, he did not dominate his actors but encouraged them to assert their own individuality, to make their own interpretations of the characters in the script. He liked to say that if you have chosen the right actors, there is little more to be done: the play is completed when they have acted their parts. He was saying that the actors are more important than the director. Greta Garbo, who depended upon her director, therefore found herself at a loss, even though Stiller was sometimes able to rehearse her privately. He was not allowed on the set and could only suggest how she should deal with each situation as it arose. Also Garbo's German was rudimentary, and Pabst could not speak Swedish.

But it was precisely because she was unnerved that she was able to play her part so well. Young, unprotected, vulnerable, she moves through the story with a trembling radiance, her beauty taking fire from her nervousness and excitability, and these were precisely the qualities Pabst demanded of her. Sometimes in the bordello scenes she seems to be completely lost and terrified, and this too was what he wanted. He did not have to direct her. All that was necessary was to let her loose in the film.

Gösta Berlings Saga celebrated the romantic past: *The Street of Sorrows* explored the unromantic present, describing the drab and bitter lives of people caught up in the postwar inflation. Here was violence, but it was not the violence of high tragedy. Pabst took over sets that were already in existence, painted them over, made them drabber. "What need is there for romantic treatment?" he said. "Real life is too romantic and too ghastly." He wanted to make films that would faithfully mirror the tragedy of his time, and he succeeded beyond all expectation because he was in sympathy with his time and had a passionate understanding of it. Today *The Street of Sorrows* has been accepted as one of the acknowledged masterpieces of cinema, and this for two reasons: Pabst's sense of passionate realism and Garbo's extraordinary beauty and delicacy as she wanders through the modern nightmare.

We shall never know exactly how *The Street of Sorrows* appeared to its first audiences, because the original prints have been lost. What survives in the Museum of Modern Art in New York is the result of the knitting together of incomplete French and Italian prints with the help of Willi Haas, the original script writer, and Marc Sorkin, the assistant director. All the scenes in which Garbo appeared have apparently survived, but there are inexplicable gaps in the last twenty minutes of the film that reduce the story to incoherence. But even in its surviving form, the film is masterly. It reeks of squalor, but it is squalor seen through the eyes of a poet: not romanticized, but made keener. For the first time the camera observed lines of poor people waiting in the icy streets for a butcher's shop to open. Stiller, with his love for Dutch painting, painted his interiors lovingly with the sunlight flooding through leaded windows. Pabst, who had grown up during the period of German expressionism, showed clammy streets drowning in the winter fog, cracked

staircases, walls slimy with grease, gaunt faces seen in the searching beams of headlights. On the Street of Sorrows it is always winter, and it is inconceivable that the sun will ever shine. If you did not know that the film was entirely made in the studio, you would think that Pabst had gone to the slums and photographed them as they were.

In the long passages where *The Street of Sorrows* tells a simple, comprehensible story, the illusion is complete. We live in that street. It is a place of the purest misery, dominated by the heavy features of Werner Krauss, the butcher, who stands guard over his small shop always accompanied by an enormous white dog, hairless and obscene. The dog curiously resembles the butcher, and you know it will leap at the throat of anyone who so much as murmurs against him. The butcher is a caricature: sleek hair parted in the middle, waxed mustache, huge muscles, a harsh and overbearing manner. He lords it over the street and sells his meat only to those who will do him favors. We recognize Garbo and the young Marlene Dietrich in the line of desperate people waiting for his shop to open. They are starving and helpless; they cringe at the sight of the butcher; they would wait all night for a piece of meat.

It is the same with the procuress, who is also a caricature, and therefore all the more effective. Valeska Gert transforms herself into a short, round-shouldered, conniving woman, with a hatchet face and a slit for a mouth, a ferocious little goblin tempting people to forbidden pleasures and demanding payment in advance. She is not simply one procuress but somehow suggests all the procuresses who have ever lived. It is a formidable performance played very quietly with exactly the right note of wheedling savagery. Canez, the South American entrepreneur with a diplomatic passport, played by Robert Garrison, is caricature gone to seed. We never quite believe in this paunchy Mephistopheles who speculates in human misery and human flesh. Black-eyed, black-browed, black-bearded, Canez stalks through the film with the air of a man who has escaped from another film and is still searching for a role. He sits back in his chair, puffs at his cigar, leers at the young women who come to offer themselves to him, and announces to his confederates that he has just thought of another way to make a fortune. All that is necessary is to spread the rumor that the miners are coming out on strike; coal shares will drop, he will buy up the shares when they have fallen to the bottom, and then, because people will pay any price for coal, he will control the market. It is a diabolical idea, but he rolls his eyes too strenuously to be believable. Asta Nielson, fine-boned and aristocratic, relishing the wealth she has accumulated by prostitution, dazzles us with a performance of chilling grandeur. She parades through the house of prostitution like an Empress, crowned with an astonishing helmet of

feathers, wearing her finery as though she was born to it. She is a credible murderess, and there are few passages in the film as moving as the passage where she realizes the enormity of her crime and all its consequences. She holds the stage by the terror of her presence, a vindictive goddess arrayed in the panoply of cruelty and remorse.

Throughout the film, with its involved story of international speculators, prostitutes, murderers, American relief officers, police agents, down-at-heel hotel keepers, and degenerates, there moves the pale, compassionate face of Garbo, forever opening like a flower, forever untouched by the vice in the dark streets. She is not innocence alone, for she knows depravity, but it is her innocence we remember. Pabst wisely shows her often in close-up. At these moments we are made aware of her innermost thoughts as we see them wandering across her face. Her freshness is something to wonder at. Here, too, there occurs, as so often in her films, the curious feeling that she is "somehow outside," like the chorus in a Greek tragedy. She is attempting to speak urgently about things that are not necessarily written in the script, things that are very deep, mysterious, and personal. Her lips move, her eyes open wide, there is the faintest inclination of her head, and suddenly we realize that she is speaking directly to us across the darkness of the cinema and the darkness of the story. In those long, steady close-ups, which directors sometimes inserted in the films without quite knowing why they did so, she seems to be speaking from the heart to the heart. We can only guess that what she is saying has something to do with her own poverty-stricken childhood and her turbulent adolescence.

There is one scene in the film that was suggested by Stiller and that derives entirely from his knowledge of the actress. It is the scene where the procuress tempts her into putting a deposit on a fur coat. Valeska Gert, the procuress, has her milliner's shop at the foot of the stairway leading to the bordello. The fur coats are on display, and every woman who enters the bordello is subject to temptation. Garbo pauses long enough in the shop to be tempted. She admires the furs, puts one on, then another, gazes at herself in the mirror, debates whether she will keep it, decides against keeping it, slides her hand over the smooth fur, smiles, takes a sidelong glance at herself in the mirror, smiles again, then confronts herself in the mirror, intoxicated by the vision of herself, by the world of luxury and ease that suddenly opens out to her. "Did I ever torture my customers for payment?" asks the procuress, her slit mouth smiling savagely, as she hovers like an embattled spider around her prey. We know, of course, that she will torture until every muscle is torn to shreds and every bone is broken. Garbo falls into the spider's web with scarcely a struggle or a sigh. It is a moment of exquisite compassion and terrible strangeness, and at the same time it is completely commonplace. At that moment innocence is forsaken, and all her past life counts for nothing in comparison with the promise of luxury represented by the gleaming fur coat. Dazed, she talks about payment, and Valeska Gert dismisses the subject as one not worth talking about. Garbo looks once more in the mirror, lost in her dream of herself. Repeatedly Pabst set her against mirrors, as Stiller set her against the snow.

There are dangers in attempting to tell the story of a film, but it is necessary to give a brief account of *The Street of Sorrows* because of its importance in the development of Garbo. The film opens with the declaration in Gothic script:

Through me the way to the Street of Sorrows:
Through me the way to eternal torment.

It is a characteristically Germanic statement, obscurely terrifying. The implication is that we are about to enter Hell, which takes the form of a dark wintry street glistening with rain, the huddled people waiting outside the butcher's shop, a one-legged ex-soldier hobbling back without food to his lodging, and when his wife asks him why he has returned empty-handed, he strikes her savagely. From the ex-soldier's hovel we move to the bourgeois comfort of Councillor Rumfort's apartment, where the only food on the table is cabbage soup. Greta Rumfort rises from the table to join the line outside the butcher's shop. Again and again the camera returns to that shop, fascinated by the devilish butcher with his hairless dog. The butcher says there is no meat, the crowd gasps, and the police break up the crowd after saluting the butcher with the deference he deserves as a powerful figure in the community. Then we see Canez, the international speculator—his unlikely full name is Don Alonso Canez—as he waddles across the floor of the Carlton Hotel and tells his army of hangers-on to spread the rumor that the Petrowicz mine workers are coming out on strike. The price of coal will go up; shares in the mining industry will go down; he will make a killing. The brilliant stratagem is applauded, and to celebrate their coming good fortune they all go off to the bordello, which takes on an increasing importance during the rest of the drama. Pabst binds these different elements together by cross-cutting. We see Canez gesticulating; then the camera cuts to the Street of Sorrows, the rain falling, the hairless dog growling and baring its teeth; Greta Rumfort returns empty-handed to her apartment; then Canez again. By these contrasting shots Pabst, a master of cutting, knits together the fates of several characters who will eventually react upon one another.

For the rest of the film Pabst is concerned with keeping afloat four or five quite separate stories. There is the story of Councillor Rumfort and his family, the story of Canez and his hangers-on, the story of the aging prostitute, the story of the murder, and the story of the love affairs of the young attorney Egon Stirner, whose role is never made quite clear in the surviving film. Stirner is an ambivalent figure, torn between the desire for a rich heiress and the desire to live virtuously. He has affairs with women, borrows money from them, finds his happiness in pursuing them and being pursued by them. Because the film is fragmentary, some important elements of his role remain unexplained even though he is essential to Pabst's purpose. Pabst was producing a morality play, with Canez and the butcher playing Mephistopheles and Satan, while Garbo plays Innocence, and Egon Stirner is a man caught in toils of his own making.

Councillor Rumfort learns from a newspaper that government employees will receive two years' salary if they voluntarily terminate their employment and relinquish all claims for the future. He is over-joyed, runs off to the government office that dispenses the money, and returns home drunk with wealth. On that same day his daughter, work-ing as a secretary, is invited to her boss's office at the top of the stairs, and while he is attempting to seduce her, she faints from hunger. She returns home to find the Councillor feasting the whole family, celebrat-ing his newfound wealth with champagne. He has bought stock in coal mines; it will increase in value, and he will become immensely wealthy. While he laughs and fusses around the table heaped with good things, his daughter looks on uncomprehendingly, waiflike, shuddering a little, for she knows that sudden wealth does not spring from the ground.

These early shots in the film have magic in them. Garbo looks at the flowers, the food on the table, the furniture in the room with a sense of quiet joy and compassion, like Eve on the morning of Creation. She walks about the house in a happy daze; she has only to run her hand along the back of a chair for us to know that it has been an intimate part of her life since childhood. In this way she gives a sense of permanence to the setting.

Her father gives her some money to buy a coat. Thus, very delicately, we are led into the tiny shop kept by the procuress. She gives the procu-ress a down payment and goes to her office, where the boss makes a second effort to seduce her; when she rejects his advances, he screams at her that she must have bought the coat out of her immoral earnings, and self-righteously dismisses her. Soon Councillor Rumfort has lost all his money. He puts up a sign: "Rooms for Rent." Garbo tries to sell back her coat. Valeska Gert smiles her most winning smile. "If you want money," she says, "I can introduce you to gentlemen of influence."

The Street of Sorrows

It is a moment of pure horror and pure triumph. Garbo succumbs, walks slowly up the stairs, finds herself in the bordello confronting Werner Krauss, who is elegant in evening dress, more terrifying than ever now that he has left his butcher's shop, his dog, and the dark street, which he rules like an emperor. But she has not succumbed to the extent that she can give herself to the enemy and abruptly flees to the safety of her apartment, where Einar Hanson has come to live in the rented room. He is no more credible than Werner Krauss; he is almost a caricature of male beauty, a waxwork with an emphatic smile and glistening eyes, neither human nor inhuman. He clicks his heels, smiles, goes through the motions of adoring her, and gives her, as a testimony of more favors to come, some canned goods from the supplies brought to Vienna by the American relief organization. It is clear that Pabst had never set eyes on an American, and the absurd heel-clicking suggests a curious insensitivity to detail. For a while there is peace and contentment in the Rumfort household. But when Greta Rumfort's young sister steals some of those precious canned goods out of despair and hunger, the American officer abruptly decides he can no longer live in such a house. He leaves none too soon, for his presence clutters the story, which is already encumbered with too many characters. Greta returns to the bordello, as the sole means of earning a living and paying off her debts.

The bordello scenes are convincing, perhaps because they are filmed on grainy stock while Garbo's scenes were filmed on the best Kodak stock available in Paris. This, too, works in favor of the finished film— the radiant, clearly visible Garbo and the ghostly wraiths disporting themselves in the bordello. Once Greta Rumfort is pursued, someone tears at her dress, her small breasts are revealed, white among the tangles of black lace, and there is the sense of a rape, of something so terrible that it can only be hinted at, and all this is brought about by the half-darkness of the grainy film. When film was perfected and an even lighting was spread over stage sets, something very precious was lost to cinema.

The Street of Sorrows belongs to the period when film was expanding its range and new techniques were being discovered. It was still fresh, still malleable. If it tended to deal in caricatures, it was because caricatures were not yet stereotyped, and sometimes the very defects of film served to give a greater reality to the events that were being portrayed. Today, looking at these early films, we wonder why we are so deeply moved watching actors who jerk to hand-turned cameras, who seem to be always running rather than walking, and whose lips form four words that are then translated by three sentences in the titles. But this world had its own conventions, and in the early 1920s even the inadequacies of film were regarded as advantages. The silence of the film allowed everyone to imagine the exact depth and timbre of the voices; the mind of the audience was working; much was left to the imagination. Garbo without her voice spoke more powerfully in those early films than she ever would again.

Stiller, who was wise and sensible when he directed films, showed himself to be totally incompetent when he began to think of himself as the promoter of an international consortium designed to produce films in several languages. Pathé in France and Ufa in Germany were contemplating an amalgamation, and Stiller imagined that half a dozen European film companies, including the Swedish Biograf, would unite and place him at their head. It was a dazzling vision; it satisfied his ego, but left him frustrated and despondent when he discovered that all his endless meetings with high officials and producers amounted to nothing more than a general expression of interest in his plan. No one put up any money. No one, not even Ivar Kreuger, the Swedish "Match King," was prepared to grant Stiller all the powers he wanted in this grandiose scheme that embraced most of Europe. Although many admired him as a director, very few regarded him as a capable administrator.

Meanwhile the one man who was able to do whatever he liked in films was gradually moving in the direction of Berlin after a few weeks in Paris and Rome. He was Louis B. Mayer, the son of a peddler in New Brunswick who had escaped from Minsk with his small family to eke out a living in Canada. When he was about twenty, Mayer became the owner of a nickelodeon in Haverhill, Massachusetts, a shoe-manufacturing city thirty miles north of Boston. He called it the Orpheum, celebrated the grand opening with a film based on the Passion Play at Oberammergau, fought off all his competitors, and gradually acquired a small empire of nickelodeons in New England. Totally unscrupulous, he began to extend his empire across America, and by 1918 he had installed himself in Los Angeles—not yet the powerful and imperious figure he would become later, but already well on the road to absolute power.

Sharp-featured, and with a mouth like a trap, Mayer was a formidable antagonist in a quarrel, and he was always quarreling. In the fall of 1924 he was quarreling with the director and actors in Rome who were making a film based on the book by General Lew Wallace called *Ben-Hur: A Tale of the Christ*. The director, Fred Niblo, and Francis X. Bushman, the perennial matinee idol, were given tongue-lashings for various crimes committed by them—Niblo was too slow, Bushman was stealing scenes from Ramon Novarro, who was one of Mayer's protégés.

Mayer went on to deliver more tongue-lashings to other people involved in the film, and set off for Berlin in good spirits.

In Berlin, as in all the other cities he visited, Mayer saw the new films, met directors and actors, and conducted himself like a reigning potentate. Because he was in fact one of the triumvirate who ruled over the recently formed organization known as Metro-Goldwyn-Mayer, and not the least of them, he felt he had a perfect right to act regally and capriciously. Victor Sjöström had suggested that he should meet Mauritz Stiller, and because Sjöström was a Hollywood director of some eminence who had left Sweden the previous year and already demonstrated that he possessed a talent for getting along with Americans, Mayer's first task in Berlin was to seek out Stiller. He imagined he would find someone as agreeable and unemotional as Sjöström. Instead he found another potentate.

Tall, lantern-jawed, immaculately dressed, Stiller presented himself as the supreme arbiter of taste, the one creative spirit left in European filmmaking. In a casual fashion he offered to show Mayer *Gösta Berlings Saga*, which they saw in a private screening room with an interpreter. When Mona Martenson appeared in an early scene in the film, Mayer commented on her beauty and the comment was translated for Stiller, who merely grunted. A little while later Greta Garbo appeared on the screen. Mayer asked for her name. Stiller roared back, "Look at the picture! Look at the direction!" He had a loud, booming voice, and Mayer was lifted half out of his seat. Thereafter Mayer watched the picture attentively and said nothing to disturb Stiller's equanimity.

When it was over he complimented Stiller for his direction and said he was impressed by the acting of Lars Hanson and of the girl whose name he had forgotten. "Greta Garbo," Stiller said. "Yes, that's right," Mayer said. He had an obscure impression that Stiller wanted to come to Hollywood, an impression that was confirmed when Stiller spoke again about the sweep and magnificence of the direction. Mayer was obviously taken with Garbo. Stiller invited him to meet her for dinner the next day at the Adlon Hotel. Mayer sent off a cable to Sjöström, saying he had met Stiller and was favorably impressed but was not sure how Stiller would react to conditions in Hollywood. What was Sjöström's opinion? Sjöström replied that Stiller was an authentic genius and he would not have the slightest difficulty getting along in Hollywood.

Stiller deliberately chose the Adlon Hotel for the first meeting between Mayer and Garbo not only because it was the most sumptuous in Berlin but also because he knew about a table where Garbo's magnificence could be displayed to best advantage. He arranged the lighting, tipped the *maître d'hôtel* and the headwaiter generously, and decided exactly where Mayer and Garbo should sit. When Mayer arrived, he was conscious that the whole affair was being stage-managed by a consummate director. Stiller was a good host, though he talked endlessly and was impatient with the translator. Mayer was fascinated by him and paid little attention to Garbo. He was on his guard. But as the dinner progressed, he came increasingly to share Sjöström's opinion. He was determined to bring Stiller, Garbo, and Lars Hanson to Hollywood, which had much to learn from Europe. Stiller was the big catch. Garbo, though obviously beautiful, was of considerably less importance. He offered Stiller a salary of $1,000 a week, whereas Garbo and Lars Hanson would receive $350 a week. Nor was Mayer in any hurry to welcome them in Hollywood, for the contract was signed in Berlin in the middle of November 1924 and it stipulated that the salaries would be paid from July 1, 1925. Mayer's last comment, as he was about to leave the table, was addressed to the interpreter: "Tell Miss Garbo that in America people don't like fat women." Garbo heard the interpreter's translation and shrugged her shoulders.

Although Mayer was struck by her beauty, he had no high hopes for her as an actress. For him, bodies counted most of all. He observed that Garbo was flat-chested, with broad hips, thick ankles, and what appeared to him to be an ungainly way of walking. Perhaps something could be made of her. In the following days he enthused over his capture of Stiller at a remarkably cheap price, and he forgot about Garbo altogether.

Meanwhile Garbo was working on *The Street of Sorrows* and beginning to assert her independence from Stiller. When the film was completed she returned to Stockholm. Stiller followed her. He was still living high, but he had no income and no prospects except the directorial job in Hollywood, which would pay no salary until July. As time passed, he became increasingly uneasy. How would they treat him in Hollywood? How much freedom would they give him? He sent off long letters to Victor Sjöström that plainly indicate that he was still undecided, nervous, edgy, and quite capable of tearing up his contract with Mayer. Sjöström counseled patience and a good-humored resignation; "the great Moje" was perfectly capable of taking Hollywood in his stride. Stiller made no films, wrote no scenarios, and gave himself up to a prolonged state of indecision.

He accompanied Garbo to the premiere of *The Street of Sorrows*, which took place in the Mozartsaal in Berlin on May 18, 1925. He looked much older, his hair was turning gray though he was only forty-two, and he was clearly not in his best form. The somber film was received rapturously by the critics, who praised the direction of Pabst—it was his second film and he was little known—and the acting of the aging Asta Nielsen and the young Greta Garbo. Stiller was pleased, for his protégée was receiving the recognition she deserved and he knew he was responsible for one of the best passages in the film, the scene where Greta Rumfort covets the luxurious fur coat and gazes at herself in the mirror with an expression of joy and bewilderment. The scene was played with great tenderness and beauty and stood out as one of the focal scenes, as memorable as the early shots of the hideous Street of Sorrows with the obscene dog and the equally obscene butcher. In Germany, Italy, France, and Spain the film was acclaimed, but it fared less well in England and least well in the United States, where the naked misery of postwar Europe was little understood.

While Stiller was a prey to indecision, Garbo was looking forward excitedly to her visit to America. She was twenty years old; already she had been a star in two important films; the future seemed to be opening out into an endless array of successes. She was too young to think of defeat and too innocent to realize that defeat was ultimately inevitable. She had learned much from Stiller and perhaps almost as much from Pabst. It never occurred to her that the miserable $350 a week she would be paid by MGM was a measure of her insignificance in the eyes of Louis B. Mayer. In her eyes it amounted to a fortune. In the eyes of Stiller, who had been contemplating his wounds, it was a grotesque insult, and he had decided to point out its absurdity to Louis B. Mayer at the first opportunity. There were days when he seemed to be a volcano about to explode. Some prophetic instinct told him that the visit to America was doomed to failure.

On a foggy day at the end of June the SS *Drottningholm* sailed out of Göteborg. Stiller and Garbo were making their first voyage on an ocean liner, and Stiller was in unusually good spirits, having decided that at least until he arrived in New York he would enjoy himself. When the *Drottningholm* slipped alongside the Swedish-American Line pier, a welcoming committee climbed aboard. It consisted of a solitary girl in Swedish costume who handed Garbo a bouquet, a public relations man from MGM, a photographer, and an interpreter. Clearly MGM did not regard their arrival as a matter of importance. The part-time photographer took four pictures and then hurried away. One of these pictures, printed the next day in the *New York Graphic*, shows Garbo and Stiller leaning against the ship's railing near a life preserver. Stiller is wearing a natty English suit and an English cloth cap, while Garbo wears a light, checkered summer dress and a cloche hat. For greater safety she has

Greta Garbo and Mauritz Stiller, July 1925

Greta Garbo and Jaro Furth

looped the handle of her black leather handbag around her wrist. She is smiling but does not look very sure of herself, and the photograph scarcely celebrates her beauty; it might be any young starlet arriving in America. There was a heat wave in New York. Everyone wanted to get out of the sun. Soon they were driven to the Hotel Commodore on Forty-second Street, where two small suites had been reserved for them by MGM. There, during one of the hottest summers on record, they remained for two months until Louis B. Mayer decided what to do with them.

Caught in the Crossfire

I do not fear you, Manos Duras.
—From *The Temptress*

IN LATER YEARS Garbo would say that the most miserable period of her career was the two months she spent at the Hotel Commodore during that sweltering summer. New York terrified her. The noise, the heat, the difficulty of communication, the strange manners of the New Yorkers, and the silence from Hollywood—all these frightened her. Nervous and irascible, Stiller marched up and down his suite like a caged beast, while Garbo spent at least half the day in her bathtub to escape the heat. Sometimes they wandered over to Times Square to see movies, but it was wasted effort, for they found nothing worth seeing.

Stiller was exasperated by Louis B. Mayer's refusal to answer his letters. Garbo did her best to smooth his ruffled feathers, but she too became disconsolate as the days passed and no news came from Hollywood. Although shy, she possessed an iron will, she was determined to become a great international star with Stiller as her director, and she refused to give way to despair.

One day during the summer, Stiller and Garbo paid a social call on Arnold Genthe, a master photographer and prodigious collector of Japanese prints. The meeting came about through Martha Hedman, a Swed-

98

ish opera singer at the Metropolitan Opera who knew Genthe well and admired his photographs. At Genthe's studio they pored over the photographs and spoke in German. Garbo liked the photographs. In his memoirs Genthe recalls Garbo saying very tentatively, "I would love to have you make some pictures of me sometime."

"Why sometime?" Genthe replied. "Why not now? You're here and I'm here and I must make some photographs of you to have visible proof that you are real."

Then she smiled, but protested earnestly, "No, not now. Look at my dress, and I don't like my hair."

"Never mind that," Genthe said. "I am more interested in your eyes and what is behind that extraordinary forehead."

Thereupon for about an hour Genthe took a series of photographs of her, some in close-up, some waist length, all of them reflecting a quivering intensity. In one, the most beautiful, she rests her chin on her hand, and the photographer has given to that hand the abrupt delicacy of a white orchid. We see only the face, the hand, a shock of wild hair; but the expression is so appealing, the face so vulnerable, the heavily lidded eyes so mysterious, the lips so full and tender that the photograph, though set in shadows and perhaps especially because it is set in shadows, conveys the essence of femininity. She is young womanhood, serene but with a hint of tragedy. There is nothing to suggest she is Swedish; she could be a young Indian girl, Persian, Arab, Jewish, German, Italian, French, American. All that is accidental has been removed, and there is only an immediately arresting, poignant, and supremely beautiful face. When Stiller lay dying in a Stockholm hospital a few years later, this was the photograph he was holding.

Genthe took other photographs of Garbo, including one that must have been taken a few moments later, for there is little change of expression, but this time she is running her hand through her hair. These photographs were later offered to Frank Crowninshield, the editor of *Vanity Fair*, who accepted the superb photograph in which she rests her chin on her hand, and printed it on the cover of his magazine with the caption, "A New Star from the North—Greta Garbo." But neither MGM nor Stiller was very hopeful about her prospects. Tests made in New York were sent to Hollywood, studied, and found wanting. Louis B. Mayer had entirely lost interest in Stiller and Garbo, who now became expendable. One day in August, Garbo called on Genthe to thank him for the set of pictures he had sent her. She looked tired and resigned. "I've come to say good-bye," she said with a sigh. "They don't seem to want me. They say I am a type. I'm going back to Berlin."

Genthe was a man of considerable resourcefulness, and well aware of his own renown as a photographer. He asked her whether she had shown his photographs to MGM. She had not. She would not have known how to go about it. Indeed, she had very little contact with MGM officials in New York. They had come to the conclusion that she belonged to a familiar type. She might be used for one or two films, and in the normal course of events she would then be quickly abandoned, like so many actresses. Stiller arranged that MGM should see Arnold Genthe's photographs, but it made no difference. Hollywood would have been quite happy if Stiller and Garbo had torn up their contracts and gone home. Stiller, however, was digging in his heels. He had a useful ally in Victor Sjöström, who finally arranged that after their two months' exile in New York, MGM should sufficiently bestir itself to invite them to Hollywood.

This time there was a real welcoming committee, but it was not from MGM. They were welcomed at the Los Angeles railroad station by two little Swedish girls with bouquets, some Swedish businessmen hastily rounded up for the occasion, two or three Swedish actors working in Hollywood, and a photographer. Garbo stood by the railroad tracks nearly smothered with flowers, wearing a blouse with a broad collar and the long heavy skirt of the period. In a picture taken by the photographer she looks very appealing as she stands between the two little girls in the hard Californian sunlight. Stiller, so long a prey to melancholy fears, looks healthy, relaxed, and good-humored. He wears a high collar, vest, and business suit and might have just stepped out of a meeting with Stockholm bankers. He is hopelessly overdressed for a California summer.

July and August had passed, and now it was September. They were both eager to work, but nothing happened. Neither of them made any impression on Hollywood, or rather they had made the kind of impression that is faintly sinister because it suggested that they were both incapable of fitting into the established pattern. Stiller was labeled "independent, aloof, difficult." Garbo was labeled "Scandinavian type, dowdy, inexperienced." Dorothy Woodridge observed Garbo's clothes closely: "Her shoes were run down at the heels. Her stockings were silk, but in one was a well-defined run. As a sartorial masterpiece she was a total loss."

There were other things told in her disfavor during her early weeks in Hollywood. She was appallingly naïve, perhaps stupid, her movements were clumsy, her feet too big; her teeth needed to be fixed; she giggled and laughed loudly, wore cheap clothes, and quite obviously was not star material. In attempting to satisfy Stiller, Louis B. Mayer had evidently committed one more of his small errors. Stiller, too, was an error. Now

Greta Garbo by Arnold Genthe

that the MGM staff had an opportunity to observe them, the general consensus was that they were not very extraordinary and could safely be disregarded. The cruel theatrical command "Don't call us, we'll call you" was sent out, and they were left to vegetate. Garbo took long solitary walks, sized up the situation, and came to the conclusion that she was young and could endure any punishment inflicted upon her because she knew in her heart that she was destined to be a great star. Stiller, who knew his time was running out, and who knew that he had done nothing of any consequence since making *Gösta Berlings Saga*, was raging more terribly than ever. He wrote scenarios in Swedish, which no one took the trouble to translate, and spent his evenings with Garbo. They sat on the terrace of the great, white, sprawling Miramar Hotel in Santa Monica, gazing out to sea in the direction of Catalina island. Sometimes they would sit for hours saying nothing, in the Swedish fashion.

What was needed was the pure unforeseeable accident, the moment when the key turns in the lock of its own accord. This finally happened for Garbo but not for Stiller. It happened when Monta Bell, a former reporter for the *Washington Herald* turned film director, was looking at some flood scenes to be used in a film based on a novel called *Entre Naranjos* by Vicente Blasco-Ibáñez. It was a very turgid novel written at the beginning of the Spanish author's career, and it had been translated into English under the title *The Torrent*. Monta Bell was looking at torrential floods when suddenly he found himself watching the screen test of Garbo, which had somehow been spliced into the film. The surprised projectionist nervously volunteered to stop the film. "No, go ahead," Monta Bell said. "I want to see her. I want that girl for *The Torrent*." He needed her because Alma Rubens, who had already been chosen for the part, had fallen ill.

Monta Bell was an intelligent but not very imaginative director who had worked as Chaplin's assistant in making *A Woman of Paris*, a tragicomedy much in advance of its time. He was so captivated by Garbo's screen test that he immediately summoned her to his office, discussed the film with her, and gave her the script to read. Preliminary work on the film had already begun, and Ricardo Cortez had been given the role of the proud landowner of Valencia who falls in love with a peasant girl on his estate only to have the love affair broken up by his even prouder and more imperious mother. In the course of time the peasant girl becomes a prima donna in Paris and has the world at her feet, with kings, princes, and grand dukes vying for her favors. But she is in love with the landowner, and when she is almost the most famous woman in the world, known as La Brunna, she returns to Valencia. Once again they declare their love for one another, although they must meet secretly because the

matriarch is firmly determined to prevent their marriage. It is at this point that the land is overwhelmed by a flood, and the hero swims out to rescue his beloved, but to no avail. She does not need rescuing, her house stands above the flood waters, and she is calmly reading a book when the hero arrives, soaked to the skin, looking more like a water rat than an acceptable screen lover. She tells him to change his clothes, nodding in the direction of the bedroom. This he does, and returns to her wearing one of her more luxurious furs, whereupon they curl up on the sofa and rather painfully discuss their ancient love affair and yearn for marriage. The old matriarch will have none of it, the hero is no hero, and the heroine returns to her career and to her adoring public. Many years later she encounters her former lover under the worst possible conditions. He has grown paunchy and has fathered two children by the wife his mother chose for him. He looks very sad and helpless, and there is something about him that reminds one of a fat insect caught on flypaper. The heroine, for no discoverable reason, is still in love with him and sings in all the capitals of Europe with a broken heart.

Such was the first film Garbo made on American soil. Without much subtlety the title writers elucidated the theme of the torrent that was "as furious and relentless as the passion which surges in the hearts of lovers." It was trite even in 1925. To see the film today is an almost unbearable experience—almost but not quite. When Garbo appears, the film flickers into life and sometimes there are sudden surges of excitement: The white face glows as though lit by candles within, and she hints at fierce youthful passions with a raw nakedness of expression that is very appealing. Ricardo Cortez, who more clearly resembles a cautious tax collector than a matinee idol, appears to disintegrate in her presence, and he was never more ridiculous than when he risks his life to rescue her, paddling furiously in his rowboat through a storm artificially created on one of the back lots of Culver City, where MGM had established its studios. He is the muscle man flaunting his strength against the worst nature can throw at him. He does not look like a Spaniard; he looks vaguely Germanic. Ricardo Cortez, the Latin lover, was in real life Jacob Krantz. Nor does Garbo look Spanish, though she wears a black wig and is seen briefly playing on a Spanish guitar and singing Spanish songs. *The Torrent* therefore has the appearance of a charade, which never touches life and demands nothing of the audience except a kind of amused acquiescence.

There are moments in the film when Garbo is still recognizably the same actress who performed in *Gösta Berlings Saga* and *The Street of Sorrows*. She has the same curious slow waywardness, as though she is waiting for something beautiful and wonderful to happen but without

Lucy Beaumont and Greta Garbo

Greta Garbo and Ricardo Cortez

Greta Garbo and Ricardo Cortez

much hope; she moves like flowing water, she absorbs a situation rather than reacts to it, and her gestures are cautious and European. By contrast the American actors move briskly and jerkily and are clearly being directed. They are told to move from A to B, lift a hand at a precise moment, to react with their bodies. Garbo raises her head a fraction of an inch and somehow suggests an entirely novel train of thought that has nothing to do with the story but is far more exciting. She is always alone, dreaming up her own life, and Ricardo Cortez becomes an intrusion or an optical illusion.

That loneliness would persist throughout her silent movies. Even in the torrid love scenes the movement and the energy flow from her, not from the lover. The absurd potato head of Ricardo Cortez lies on her lap, and she broods over it, radiant as the full moon, and we are given the illusion that something exciting is happening. If she had brooded over a potato, we would have had the same feeling.

Although Monta Bell was directing her on the set, she was in fact still being directed by Stiller. Night after night she went to his apartment to be coached, to learn, to study. Garbo was learning English quickly, but Stiller found it virtually impossible to speak more than a few gutteral words. Sven Hugo-Borg, an accomplished and kindly interpreter, would translate for her the scenes to be played before the camera the following day, and Stiller would then pretend he was Monta Bell and explain exactly how he wanted it performed. Stiller's sense of style was reflected in her performance, and it was due to him that she was completely convincing as the world-renowned diva, the singer known as La Brunna.

In those days films were made quickly. Begun in the middle of November, *The Torrent* was completed by Christmas. The studio executives trooped into the projection room with their usual boredom and indifference. Someone asked whether Garbo was present; she was not. But Stiller was there, towering over everyone else, watching closely and sitting very upright, determined not to miss a moment of this strange film, which, though irretrievably ruined by the absurdity of the story, contained some passages of great beauty. Louis B. Mayer silenced the rather negative comments of his colleagues. "The picture," he announced, "is holding my interest." He was agreeably surprised by Garbo's acting and was well aware that Stiller was largely responsible for the quality of her performance. It was decided that if *The Torrent* was well received by the public, Stiller would be permitted to direct her in another film.

The New York premiere took place on February 21, 1926. The name of Ricardo Cortez, an established star, came first, but it was Garbo who drew the applause of the critics. "The girl has everything, with looks,

Sincerely -
Greta Garbo -

acting ability, and personality," wrote *Variety*. "When one is a Scandinavian and can put over a Latin characterization with sufficient power to make it most convincing, need there be any more said regarding her ability?" Indeed, there was much more to be said, and the reviewers said it at considerable length. A new star had risen. Exactly how she differed from other stars was a matter of discussion. Several reviewers pointed out that she seemed to contain within herself elements of many other stars, so that it was possible to detect in her acting and in her appearance some vestiges of Gloria Swanson, Norma Talmadge, Zasu Pitts, Carol Demster, and other stars. In fact MGM had been forcing her to see a great number of films, and she found herself unconsciously mimicking other actresses. Seeing the film today, we are less aware of mimicry because we no longer remember how Gloria Swanson, Norma Talmadge, and the others acted in their early films. The general consensus of the critics was that Garbo was a person in her own right with vast and exciting possibilities.

Stiller was now in favor. He had written a script, based on a Blasco-Ibáñez novel called *La Tierra de Todos*, which had been received favorably by Louis B. Mayer and his chief of staff, Irving Thalberg. Unhappily his script was sent to the script department, which decided for its own reasons to edit it and change the story line. Stiller objected strenuously, but he was one man against a firmly entrenched bureaucracy. What especially appalled him was that Garbo was transformed into a *femme fatale* who destroyed men with her seductive glances and ended, as she deserved, in the gutter. The setting was the Argentine. Instead of rising flood waters and a heroic rescue by rowboat, a dam would burst and there would be heroic rescues by other means. There would also be a peculiarly ferocious duel with the antagonists armed with bullwhips. Stiller was appalled by this story but felt that, as a director, he could impose his own poetry and his own sense of direction on it, subtly transforming it, even while he followed the script. He once said that any woman plucked off the street could be transformed into an actress. Less convincingly he also said that any story could be transformed into a great film. MGM decreed that the film should be called *The Temptress* and watched with some trepidation as Stiller took command of the actors and launched into his first directorial job since his arrival in America.

From the beginning there seemed to be a curse on the picture. Tempers were ragged, Stiller's limited English failed him, he shouted "Go" when he meant "Stop," lost his temper, and looked more like a caricature of a great director than like an artist who had directed forty films, some of them masterpieces. He complained of the number of people

Publicity stills for The Torrent

standing around the set. What were they doing? They were stand-ins, script girls, supervisors, head-office factotums. He ordered them off the set, but they remained. Garbo was terrified. She could feel the mounting pressure against Stiller, and there were other things to be terrified about. One morning Stiller called her aside and gently showed her a telegram just received from Stockholm, saying that her sister, Alva, had died. Her death was sudden and completely unexpected. The story was told that when Garbo saw the telegram, she said, "There's nothing we can do, Moje. We must go back on the set." The story was untrue. She collapsed and was taken home, but was back on the set the next day.

Although Louis B. Mayer was the kingpin around which the organization revolved, the day-to-day operations of the studio were firmly in the hands of Irving Thalberg, the "boy genius," who was regarded as infallible. Nervous, abrupt, and excitable, conscious of his own glory and capable of making earth-shaking decisions whenever the mood came over him, he had no great opinion of Garbo and no understanding of Stiller, who was ordered off the set ten days after he had begun shooting. He was incensed but without recourse. Thereafter Thalberg would have nothing more to do with him. His place as director of *The Temptress* was taken by Fred Niblo, who had directed *Ben-Hur*, the extravaganza that had caused Louis B. Mayer so much trouble during his visit to Rome. Niblo was a man who could be relied upon not to say "Stop" when he meant "Go."

Garbo was now caught in the crossfire. In time Thalberg would revise his opinion of her and declare that he alone was responsible for her great talent and enduring fame, but he was mistaken. He made things impossibly difficult for her during the making of *The Temptress* and drove her very close to a nervous breakdown. Stiller, the one man who understood her, her only real confidant, and the only person who really knew the prodigious things she was capable of doing, was publicly disgraced. He would make a few more films of no importance and then die heartbroken in a charity ward in a Stockholm hospital.

In private Garbo complained bitterly against her treatment by MGM. She had no illusions about its cause and understood much better than Thalberg what had gone wrong. It was more than a clash of personalities or a clash of styles. It was quite simply that Hollywood would not tolerate the presence of a genius like Stiller and would destroy him if possible. If, by some remarkable accident, a genius like Charlie Chaplin was able to survive, it was not by virtue of any encouragement from Hollywood but by the sheer force of his character and his staying power. Charlie Chaplin defied Hollywood, but Hollywood finally succeeded in ridding itself of him. It was not very difficult. A trumped-up morals

charge and the accusation that he was a Communist were sufficient. With Mauritz Stiller it was even easier. All that was necessary was to spread the rumor that he was a "difficult man to get along with" and that he was "slow and finicky."

Garbo now had to confront the fearful stupidities of Hollywood alone. The publicity people of MGM took command of her, posed her beside a tame lion, placed a tiger cub in her arms, stripped her down to a jersey and shorts and photographed her surrounded by muscular track stars from the University of Southern California. In the same costume she was photographed with Dean Cromwell, a famous track coach of the period, as she was about to sprint the half-mile. Dean Cromwell holds a starter's gun in his hand and looks as though he is going to shoot her. In these publicity shots she resembles a unicorn set amid wild donkeys.

The Temptress was saved from disaster by the cameraman, William Daniels, who had photographed *The Torrent* and would photograph nearly all her films. He was fascinated by the subtleties of her expression and made prolonged experiments with lighting until he caught exactly the effects he wanted. Throughout her film career she was very close to him, giving him presents, remembering his birthday, recognizing him as a professional, while the directors usually gave the appearance of being amateurs.

The story, being an adaptation of an adaptation, belongs to the realm of higher lunacy. Elena, the Marquise Fontenoy, suffers from an unappeasable hunger for men, whom she destroys one by one. The Marquis himself is the least of her conquests, and she goes out of her way to remind him at a masked ball that she is finished with him. As she whirls through the masked dancers and inexplicably finds herself among a small army of revelers in clowns' costumes, we realize that she is in full pursuit of Robledo, a well-established and enterprising engineer from Argentina. They remove their masks, fall in each others' arms, and are immediately engulfed in a passionate romance. Because Robledo is a stuffed shirt, it is not apparent why she is attracted to him. Robledo, acted by Antonio Moreno, is one more of those improbable lovers whose presence in Garbo's arms can only be accounted for by assuming that the man who cast them had never previously seen them together.

The story is set in Paris and Argentina, neither of them very convincing, both of them having been constructed of tar paper and white plaster. In Paris Garbo descends staircases; in the Argentine she does the same. The men who stand at the foot of the stairs are awed by her when they first see her, and they are driven mad before she is halfway down. She is depicted as a woman with an icy contempt for men, but every movement of her body and every glance suggest otherwise. Why has she

ruined so many lives? She replies, or rather the printed title says, that men have never wanted her for herself but only for her body. This is not very convincing. When she comes to Argentina, still pursuing Robledo, we are a little surprised to find him gazing at her disinterestedly, more concerned with building his dam and superintending the work of his peasants than with making love to her. She stays in his house. Manos Duras, the local bandit, having heard of her beauty, attempts to serenade her and carry her off on his horse. The bandit taunts Robledo into fighting a duel with bullwhips. This could have been the best part of the film, but the whips are made of silk and the wounds have obviously been painted on. "I do not fear you, Manos Duras," Elena says when the bandit takes her roughly in his arms. This is a moment of great danger, but the duel is less exciting than the face of Elena as she peers from an upper window at the duelists in the courtyard below, no more dangerous to men than the white face of the moon, smiling benignly, and almost too beautiful to be believed.

It is odd that Spain and Argentina were the locales of her first two films in America. It is as though they felt an obscure compulsion to strain the credulity of the audience, to place her in the most unlikely setting, to heap impossible burdens on her. She thrived on these artifices. Only the male characters, though present on the screen, seem so inconsequential that they appear to have no real existence. Inevitably Manos Duras swears revenge. Inevitably he blows up the dam. Inevitably he leaves a message for Elena: "My songs could not touch your heart—perhaps a symphony in dynamite will be more to your liking." Robledo struggles to shore up the ruins of the dam in a night of darkness and horror. He goes up to her room, determined to kill her because she is the cause of all their miseries, but he does not kill her. Instead they fall into an embrace, and the film might quite logically have ended there, but instead she slips away during the night, leaving him to his beloved dam, and departs for Paris.

Six years later Robledo, top-hatted, elegantly attired, and accompanied by his new wife, visits Paris. In a sidewalk café he encounters the former *femme fatale* sitting at a marble-topped table. She stares drably in front of her, not recognizing him. "Don't you know me?" he says. "I have met so many men," she replies hopelessly. "Elena, isn't there anything I can do?" "Yes, buy me a drink." She looks up helplessly, and it seems to her that the bearded Robledo is Christ, who is gazing at her compassionately while judging her for a life devoted irremediably to evil. Garbo and an accusing Christ! It is an extraordinary confrontation, but happily lasts only the time it takes for her to lift her head, remove the ruby ring from her finger, and offer it to him because, she says, "You died for love." And then the face of Christ dissolves into the putty face

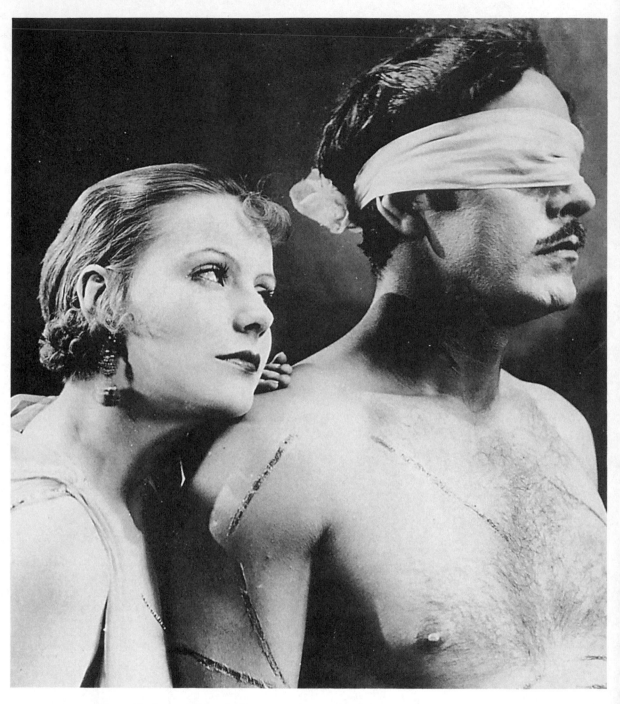

Greta Garbo and Ricardo Cortez

of Antonio Moreno, who has swashbuckled through the film, wearing a cockscomb and high-heeled riding boots, rigid as a plaster cast, elegant only when stripped to the waist, his chest crisscrossed with painted wounds which do not in the least resemble the jagged wounds caused by a bullwhip. Christ vanishes; Antonio Moreno remains.

The Temptress is a spectacular film, or rather a film full of spectacles. We see the dam breaking, the floods pouring over the land, the life of the pampas, the peasants driving carts with ten-foot-high wheels, the painted duel, wild revels at the beginning followed by a dinner given by the Marquis Fontenoy for a hundred guests. Here and there we can still detect the influence of Stiller. Where *The Torrent* possesses a kind of directness of statement and tells a more or less intelligible story, *The Temptress* suffers from a coarseness of fiber, a chaotic script, and a curious unwillingness to settle down to storytelling, for it is continually branching away into mythologies. Thus Manos Duras becomes the horny-handed Devil, provoker of evil, captain of the hosts of Hell. Robledo, touchingly good-natured, becomes Christ. Garbo, comforting him, becomes Mary Magdelen, or dressed in white, with a white lace cap and a stiff white Venetian collar, she becomes briefly the Virgin Mary with Robledo kneeling imploringly at her feet. These religious overtones were introduced into the script whenever it seemed to be failing. That the film was also intended to convey a moral is indicated by the opening statement, quoted from the Indian sage Rabindranath Tagore: "Oh, Woman! Thou art not alone the Creation of God—but of men!"

Garbo hated the film when it was finished, and Stiller was so shattered by the misuse of his protégée's talents that he threatened to sue MGM. *The Temptress* was, as Stiller knew, extremely harmful to Garbo, who would henceforward be typed as a vamp. She was to play the role of the alluring, destructive, conscienceless woman almost to the end of her film career.

To friends in Sweden Garbo apologized for the film. She wrote, "Terrible, the story, Garbo, everything is so rotten. It is no exaggeration —I was beneath criticism." But when the film was shown at the Capitol Theatre in New York on October 10, 1926, she was acclaimed by the reviewers, who paid very little attention to the story but concentrated on her poise, her grace, her beauty, and her acting. The *New York Times*, the *New York Herald Tribune*, and the *New York Mirror* were equally ecstatic. Robert E. Sherwood, writing in the old *Life*, pronounced her the "official Dream Princess" and spoke of the "efficacy of her allure." All wondered at her beauty, and no one seemed to care very much what she did or where the story led her. It was enough to look at her and enjoy her presence.

For Garbo, and for Stiller, *The Temptress* was a harrowing experience. Garbo remembered it as a picture associated with doom, for her
sister Alva, a promising actress, had died while she was making it. Alva
was only twenty-two. She had small parts in three Swedish films and
hopes of a leading part in a forthcoming film. She died of galloping consumption. When Garbo returned to Sweden she sought out the films in
which her sister had appeared and was bemused to see a dead woman
come to life again on the screen.

Although Stiller was given no work by MGM and was ostracized, he
was still on salary according to the three-year contract he had signed
with Louis B. Mayer. He was heartbroken by the treatment he received,
and he was gradually drifting away from Garbo. But there were many
in Hollywood who recognized his genius for filmmaking, and gradually,
as he came out of his depression, he began to move about, to be seen, to
talk about his plans, and to discuss the scripts he had shown to MGM,
only to be told that they were not American enough, which was true, or
incompetently written, which was untrue. One of these scripts, based on
the play *Hotel Stadt Lemberg* by the Hungarian dramatist Lajos Biro,
concerned a run-down hotel in Poland in World War I, where a cham-
bermaid, Anna Sedlak, hides and falls in love with an officer of the Austro-Hungarian Army. Stiller pointed out that the part of the chamber-
maid would serve as an admirable vehicle for Garbo. MGM was not
interested. Erich Pommer at Paramount thought it would serve as an
admirable vehicle for Pola Negri. Stiller moved from MGM to Paramount, made the film under a new title, *Hotel Imperial*, and showed that
he had lost none of his cunning. The opening scenes showing the strag-
glers of the Austro-Hungarian Army marching through the night mists
and the coming of the dispirited officer to the hotel are among the best
he ever made, and *Hotel Imperial* was a prodigious success. But there
were no more successes. *A Woman on Trial* and *Barbed Wire*, both
starring Pola Negri, were failures. He worked on one more film in Hollywood. Based on a script by Joseph von Sternberg, it told an improbable story about a London gangster who falls in love with a Salvation
Army girl and rescues her from a fire. Stiller adored fires but had only
very hazy notions about London. He began to direct the film, but fell ill
and abruptly returned to Stockholm.

This was the end, and he knew it. White-haired, his face deeply lined,
suffering atrociously from rheumatism, his shoulders and his hands shak-
ing, he returned to Sweden to die. He was a man of presentiments. He
had a presentiment when he set out for America that the trip would be a
disaster for him and a triumph for Garbo, and so it was. He had a premonition that Einar Hanson would be killed in a car accident, and on

June 3, 1927, Hanson lost control of his automobile on the Pacific Coast Highway at Santa Monica, a few moments after leaving a dinner party given for Stiller and Garbo, and was killed. "Fate has been playing dumb jokes on me," Stiller complained, and he sometimes wondered what might have happened if he had resisted the temptations of America and continued to make films in Sweden.

In the fall of 1928 he was so ill that he was taken to a hospital, and once more he had a premonition—that he would never leave it alive. Victor Sjöström visited him in the hospital. Stiller wept like a child, drank champagne from a sherry glass, spoke vaguely about some important projects that lay in the future, and when the nurse came to say the visitor must leave, he became desperate. His face was wet with tears, he clung to Sjöström and refused to be separated from him. "I want to tell you a story for a film," Stiller said. "It will be a great film; it is about human beings, and you are the only person who can make it!" The nurse was implacable. "It is time to leave," she said, and Sjöström just had time to say, "I will come in the morning, and then you will tell me the story." Stiller was weeping in the arms of the nurse, still desperately reaching out to his visitor.

When Sjöström arrived at the hospital the next morning, Stiller was scarcely able to talk. He looked fixedly at his friend, but no intelligible words came from him. He died on the following day. It was November 8, 1928, and he was only forty-five years old. In his arms, as he lay dying, he held Arnold Genthe's photograph of Garbo made soon after their arrival in New York.

There was no will; he died bankrupt and left no estate. He was buried in the North Cemetery of Stockholm in a section reserved for Jews. Some months later his family wrote to Garbo, asking her whether there was any piece of his furniture she would like as a keepsake. She chose the heavy oak chair that had once stood in the hallway of his house. It was the chair she had sat on while waiting for the first interview with him, which launched her on her career.

Flesh and the Devil

My boy, when the Devil cannot
reach you through the spirit, he
creates a woman beautiful enough
to lead you into temptation.
                —From *Flesh and the Devil*

Examined closely, John Gilbert was not quite the perfect matinee idol. He had bulbous eyes, a pudgy nose, a thin neck, and teeth that appeared to be carved out of the finest Carrara marble. He had a curious strutting walk and he talked in a thin falsetto. Yet he was undeniably handsome in a rakish way and carried himself with the air of a man who was prepared to blast his way through all obstacles. He was perhaps half-mad and more than a little desperate. He seemed in the eyes of MGM the ideal foil for the cool and reserved Garbo.

The decision was reached after long and careful deliberation, for at this time Gilbert was receiving $10,000 a week and was the most valuable property on the lot. Failure was not to be thought of. Garbo was still a somewhat doubtful property, and the new picture would have to depend largely on Gilbert's proved popularity. He had been magnificent in *The Merry Widow*, directed by Erich von Stroheim, and he had been a credible jaunty and good-hearted doughboy in *The Big Parade*, which had made more money for MGM than any previous film. What was needed now was a love story of great intensity. The choice fell unexpectedly on a turgid romance by Hermann Sudermann called *The Undying Past*.

It was a very odd choice, for even the most casual reader of Sudermann's romance would wonder how a film could be made from the story
of two young German aristocrats drowning in sentimentality, and Benjamin Glazer's screenplay meandered more incoherently than the novel.
Nor did Clarence Brown with his heavy-handed direction help the film
to run smoothly. He said later that he had never had an easier film to
direct, but he was often caught up in the drab sentimentality of the
script and made it more viscous than was necessary. We can almost hear
the voice of the director saying, "Miss Garbo, you will now throw
yourself into a tantrum—fling your hands up in the air—show yourself
plagued by the devil!" Garbo obeyed, but she was far more effective
when she showed emotion with the flicker of an eyelid, a sudden sidelong glance, or a sullen pursing of the lips.

There are moments in *Flesh and the Devil* of extraordinary power and
beauty, but they owe more to the cameraman, William Daniels, than to
the director. Daniels insisted on taking close-ups even when Brown
wanted to take medium or long shots. For the first time her face, hitherto tentatively explored, acquired dimension and authority. There had
been glimpses of this authority before, especially in *Gösta Berlings Saga*,
but now at last the study of her features becomes almost the main subject of a film. And so at intervals throughout the film the camera hovers
over her pale and luminous face, examines it minutely, moves from this
side to that; shadows are thrown upon her face, light blasts it, and all its
minute particulars are examined and displayed for our adoration. Nothing quite like this had been done before. Today when we are accustomed to seeing a single immensely magnified eye or a pair of lips on a
forty-foot screen, we take magnification in our stride, but it was not so
in those days. Daniels saw that her rare beauty permitted magnification
to the utmost degree. When we see the film today we have the odd sensation, whenever Garbo appears in close-up, of returning to a familiar
landscape where everything is known and yet there are still some details
that deserve to be studied more closely, as though it were the task of the
camera to observe her face, while all the rest of the film remained an
irrelevant shadow play.

This was a new Garbo, related distantly to the Garbo of *Gösta Berlings Saga* and *The Street of Sorrows*, but now refined by sorrow and a
greater awareness of the world's miseries. Written on her face was the
death of Alva and the knowledge that she was irremediably separated
from Mauritz Stiller. There was something of the child in that face, but
more of the mature woman—the face of someone who has emerged
from tragedy and knows she will encounter tragedy again. She was like
one of those masks fashioned for Kabuki players or Alaskan Indians,

painted white to suggest the divinity glowing within it. And there are times in *Flesh and the Devil* when her features are stern and terrible, suggesting the presence of superhuman forces that neither the camera nor the human mind can cope with.

Even at this time people were conscious that something had been let loose on the screen that bewildered and fascinated them. The face of Garbo appeared, and while it was there, you were aware of nothing else. Whatever flowed through her veins, it was not blood. The first long close-up, and the most memorable, took place at night in a garden by the light of a match that Gilbert held up to her face. In the flare of the match the lips were pale, there were heavy shadows ringing her eyes, and in this light she stared ghostlike at the camera. In fact the scene, which was set up with great care, was completely artificial. Gilbert struck a real match, but at that very moment a stagehand set light to a magnesium flare, and Garbo was blinded by it. The audience saw a face frozen into immobility, with grotesque shadows, staring blindly, transfixed into stone. What the audience saw and guessed at during this sustained passage was something akin to death: a face like a skull, made all the more terrifying because only a few moments before she had been turning the cigarette sensually in her lips. They had been dancing. Overcome by their passion, they slipped away into a garden. Gilbert asked: "Who are you?" She answered evasively. It was at this moment that Gilbert gave her the cigarette, which she rolled between her lips and put in his mouth. Then, after he had held the match for a long time, she blew it out. "You know," he says, "when you blow out the match, it is an invitation to kiss you."

There were to be many more suggestive passages in the film, but the theme had been announced, and as so often happens, the first elucidation of the theme was the best. When Garbo falls into his arms, the act of seduction appears to be complete, and the uncanny power of film to suggest the fulfillment of a sexual experience even when the lovers are only kissing comes into full play, so that it is hardly necessary to show Garbo in the following scene lying at full length on a couch with Gilbert's head on her lap and sexual exhaustion written all over their faces. But the scene is done well. Once more the camera hovers close to her face. Gilbert has never looked handsomer, and Garbo never more voluptuous, dressed now in an embroidered silk gown with the loops of embroidery rippling and cascading like the light on a damascened blade. Previously we have seen her in heavy black furs and in the white tulle she wore in the garden, but in this embroidered gown she resembles a Queen arrayed in majesty. The scene is played with superb tenderness. There is a flash of white arms; Garbo's head bends down; they kiss slowly and hungrily.

But there is no stabbing shock of recognition between lovers. They have slaked their passion and are prepared to continue because there is no end to it. It is important to observe that all this is merely the prolongation of the scene wherein Garbo appeared ghostlike in the flash of light from the magnesium flare. That scene was like an apparition, where everything necessary had been said and all the rest was decoration.

The love scene, with its casual violence, was memorable but not because of Gilbert's presence in it. As always in the scenes where Garbo plays the beloved, the lover appears to be hopelessly inadequate, however handsome and desirable he is. He becomes merely the empty vehicle of the passions of the male members of the audience, and his emptiness demands to be filled. This happened again and again. Her lovers remain shadowy; they are admitted to her presence; they make the appropriate gestures of adoration; then they vanish, leaving the male members of the audience the satisfaction of pursuing their own fantasies, while the female members identify themselves with the goddess.

Something very new was happening to films when Garbo emerged in close-up. It was both complex and very simple: complex because the audience was not accustomed to apparitions of beauty and reacted in unpredictable ways, and simple because there was about this image the quality of finality. Previously the closest the film had come to apparitional beauty was when Rudolph Valentino emerged in *The Eagle* as the romantic lover raised to the height of supreme beauty. He was, or seemed to be, Apollo incarnate, and to the audience nothing mattered except his face and his strange gliding movements. His adventures, his rages, his women were quickly forgotten. There remained the haunting face, the grace and style of his presence. Clarence Brown, who directed him, had the intelligence to recognize that the longer the camera was directed upon Valentino the better, and it scarcely mattered what he did. If he simply lay back against a pillow and smiled, the audience would know why he was smiling, and if it did not know, would invent sufficient reasons. Meanwhile the sight of Valentino's head on the pillow was itself dramatic and could be prolonged against all reason. The prolonged and apparently meaningless close-up, the close-up for its own sake, had come into existence. With Garbo, these close-ups became part of the stock in trade of filmmaking. They were inevitable, eagerly expected, and memorable, they could be inserted at random, for what people remembered afterward was rarely the story. They remembered the beautiful face in which they could read whatever they pleased.

Flesh and the Devil was notable for the large number of prolonged close-ups it contains. There were seven in *The Street of Sorrows*, five in

The Temptress, and four in *The Torrent*. There were twelve in *Flesh and the Devil*. Thereafter Garbo's directors would sometimes insert close-ups to relieve the tedium of an infantile story. They discovered, to their surprise, that a motion picture was sometimes most effective when there was no visible motion, when in fact all visible motion ceased and the audience saw the thoughts moving shadowless across a beautiful face.

With the possible exception of *Romance, Flesh and the Devil* was the most stupid film Garbo ever played in. The script, written by Benjamin Glazer, was incoherent where it was not absurd. Sudermann's romance dealt with the classic theme of the sins of the fathers being visited on the children, but the script writer transformed it into a story of jealousy set amid Teutonic mists with flashbacks into the mysterious past where improbable children swear improbable oaths amid the same rococo lakes and temples that used to be painted as backdrops in photographers' studios. Almost nothing in the film corresponded to ascertainable reality. It did not matter. Garbo's presence would have ennobled it even if it had been played backward.

The story begins in a barracks. Leo von Harden (John Gilbert) is a roué who has been spending the night on the town. At dawn, when it is discovered that he has not returned to his bunk, his comrade, Ulrich von Eltz (Lars Hanson), decides to place a pair of boots and some washbowls under Gilbert's blanket, so that he will appear to be sleeping if there is a general inspection. Hanson runs off to the parade ground in fear and trembling. He has done all he possibly can for his friend, but Gilbert can expect to be severely punished if the ruse is discovered. We see the parade ground with hundreds of soldiers in line, and Hanson loyally shouts "Present" when his friend's name is called. Then comes the inspection of the barracks and the audience is led to believe that the choleric general will find the pair of boots and the washbowls when he inspects Gilbert's bunk. Hanson rolls his eyes in terror. The general strides grimly to the bed, but when the blanket is whipped away, we discover that the real Gilbert is there, complaining that he is unwell. The general is sympathetic and is about to march out of the barracks when he observes Gilbert and Hanson jumping about hilariously, clapping each other on the back, proud of their success in outwitting the old fool. But the general is not quite as incompetent as they thought. Having seen them, he advances on them in fury and, as a punishment, consigns them to gathering up the manure in the stables. The scene ends with the two young comrades holding their noses as they wheel the manure carts.

This is not a particularly impressive beginning. It is played for laughs and establishes nothing except the fact that Gilbert and Hanson are friends, that Gilbert sometimes spends a night on the town, and that they are both army officers. It is a very odd curtain raiser for a film designed as Garbo's major introduction to America.

Happily, Garbo is not concealed for very long. Gilbert and Hanson arrive at the baroque railroad station near Hallowitz Castle, the ancestral home of the von Hardens. They are on furlough, looking forward to a good deal of dancing, drinking, and merrymaking. Garbo steps out of the train, wonderfully elegant and wonderfully beautiful. This first shot of her magnificently conveys a sense of fatality. Wrapped in heavy furs, serene and formidable, set apart from the world, descending from the train as though she were descending from outer space, she appears only briefly, though long enough to make an enduring impression. Gilbert is half-stunned by the apparition and overjoyed when she drops a white rose from her bouquet. He picks it up, clasps it, receives from her one of those brief, tentative smiles that are calculated to tear a man's heart apart, and follows her as she takes her place in a waiting carriage, offering to return the flower. Once more she smiles at him, but she gives him no further encouragement, and the carriage drives off to no one knows where. "She must be one of the guests arriving for the ball at Stoltenhof," says Gilbert's mother quite unnecessarily, for there can be no plausible explanation for the apparition. It is a wild guess, and the audience knows better.

We see no more of Garbo for a while, for Gilbert, Hanson, Gilbert's mother, and Hertha Prochvitz, the childhood sweetheart of Gilbert and Hanson, drive to Hallowitz Castle. They are ferried across a lake, and through the distant mists they see a mysterious island. "That's just Schmiz Island," says Gilbert's mother. It is one more example of her incapacity to describe things as they are. For Gilbert and Hanson it is the Island of Friendship, the place where they celebrated their childhood loyalties. There is a flashback to the steps of an antique temple on the island where, as children, they swore eternal loyalty to each other by cutting their wrists with a knife and then joining them together so that the blood mingled. "By this rite," they declaim, "we are united in riches and in poverty, in health and in sickness, in undying friendship for ever." This exhibition of *Bruderschaft* has a preculiarly German quality suitable for young stormtroopers but is not very convincing. Mist and smoke drift over the antique pasteboard temple, and a ten-year-old Hertha watches with what appears to be total incomprehension. Mercifully the two boys performing this rite in sailor suits have very little resemblance to Gilbert and Hanson, with the result that the flashback appears to be nothing more than a dreary little interlude inserted to delay the appearance of Garbo. The flashback comes to an end, and the two officers continue their journey to Hallowitz Castle. Hanson, who presumably lives in a neighboring castle, bids Gilbert farewell with a flourish. The camera now concentrates on Gilbert being received by an army of retainers. They are lined up by a major-domo, but the paunch of one of them sticks out. The major-domo pushes the paunch in and then sights along the back of the group and discovers a bottom sticking out. It is that kind of scene—rather obviously written by the same man who devised the opening scene. Then we are in Hallowitz Castle, all Hollywood gothic with baroque facings and Gilbert strutting merrily in his ancestral home.

The first love scene explodes soon afterward at the ball, when Gilbert and Garbo dance out of the ballroom into the garden. The love affair is pursued anonymously. A few days later he will learn that she has a name, Felicitas, and a husband, Count von Rhaden, who appears suddenly, having dropped from the clouds, while they are in each other's arms. In the normal course of events he could be expected to tiptoe away and take the advice of his lawyer, but Count von Rhaden is a man who believes in honor and duty. He slaps Gilbert across the face with his glove, thus ensuring that the honorable steps will be taken one by one: seconds will be appointed; a battleground will be selected; the duel will be fought. None of this is remotely believable, but it does not matter. When we see Garbo again, she is wearing a widow's weeds. She is an unconvincing widow, but wears her widowhood with aplomb. Clearly she is in love with Gilbert and has never been more voluptuous and desirable. Gilbert, however, has learned that the love affair is over. He has been ordered by the military court to serve for five years in German Southwest Africa as a punishment for engaging in a duel. They swear eternal love to each other, and in the eyes of Gilbert, which resemble billiard balls, there is a look of hopeless despair. He departs for Africa. The debonair roué finds himself incongruously in the desert among palm trees, and it would appear that he is Africa's sole inhabitant.

I have attended showings of *Flesh and the Devil* when Gilbert's departure for Africa was greeted with sustained applause, and when he first appeared in German tropical uniform there were shouts of derisive laughter. It is not quite fair. If Gilbert is improbable as Garbo's lover, he is still more improbable as a German officer in Southwest Africa. He appears to accept his fate with good grace, and this is the best that can be said for him.

The laughter stops abruptly when we see the widowed Garbo, the epitome of grief, gazing out of a window delicately patterned with falling rain, and these patterns, falling on her face, provide the tears she cannot summon. The scene is carefully orchestrated so that the waving reflections of the raindrops have the effect of giving her a strange, submarine character. Her face is still, the raindrops are in motion and animate her face, and we are almost tempted to believe she is grief-stricken. It is one of the most wonderful shots ever taken of her: the grave and serene face, the veil of raindrops, the sense of dissolution. She will melt; she will become rain; she will become air and light and water. The cameraman has invoked the elemental quality of her face.

While we are still gazing at her, the comic genius who presides over Hollywood films has commanded that Lars Hanson, Gilbert's brother officer, should make his appearance. He has come to comfort her in the loneliness of her widowhood. "I am here on behalf of my dearest friend," he says. "Is there anything I can do to lighten your grief? If you should ever need anyone to advise you, if you should ever need money. I am rich, and my purse is Leo's." To put him out of his misery she offers him a cigarette. His hands tremble, and when he strikes a match it flares up in his hand. We are led to understand that his passion has been kindled, that she will become his wife or mistress, and that both of them are doomed.

Poor Gilbert, lost in the wastes of Africa! Fortunately the Kaiser, in his great mercy, has offered him a reprieve, and the long journey from Africa is accomplished in an astonishingly brief time by the simplest of means—a long shot of a ship on the high seas followed by a close shot of train wheels. "Felicitas! Felicitas!" say the train wheels, while the face of Garbo hovers over them. Gilbert arrives at the railroad station to find Garbo and Hanson forming a welcoming party. "Welcome home, Herr von Harden," says Garbo, while Hanson pours salt on the wound with the words "She has freely forgiven you for that tragic duel." It is clear that Hanson and Garbo are married, and Gilbert is left out in the cold.

If the story must continue, there can be only one direction, a renewed love affair between Garbo and Gilbert. This is stage-managed with ease when Garbo invites him to a secret rendezvous on the Island of Friendship. Pastor Voss, who resembles the Devil, with carved beak and pointed eyebrows, curling lips and Mephistophelian gestures, pleads with Gilbert to resist temptation. "My boy, when the Devil cannot reach us through the spirit," he says, "he creates a woman beautiful enough to lead you into temptation!" He urges purity, sacrifice, abstention. Gilbert wrestles with his conscience, but not for long. Garbo appears in church, and Pastor Voss, more Mephistophelian than ever, assails her for her wantonness. She has been seen painting her lips in church; she is evidently trifling with her husband's affections; she is the Whore of Babylon. Her love for Gilbert continues, driving him to despair and joy. Having announced that he cannot tolerate duplicity and sees only one way to end the matter—he will shoot himself—he promptly takes her in his arms when she announces that she will also kill herself, dying with him for the sake of the great love they have for one another. A few moments later, as his conscience presses down on him, he attempts to strangle her. The melodrama is played stridently, with much jerking of elbows, and is no more convincing than similar melodramas played in 1860. Inevitably the guilty ones are found out. Inevitably Pastor Voss threatens them with Heaven's punishment. Inevitably Hanson learns that Garbo has been behaving improperly. Inevitably there is a duel on the Island of Friendship, or at least we are led to believe a duel is about to take place. Garbo is the last to hear about it. We see her running across the ice; cut to the duelists; return to Garbo; cut to the duelists again, then to Garbo, a white wraith stumbling across endless ice floes. The duelists have concluded that for the sake of their ancient friendship they should abandon the duel. Garbo falls through the ice. She is drowned. From time to time marvelous shapes emerge from the dark waters where the ice has broken. A sheet of paper? Her underclothes? Portions of a tablecloth? She does not come up for a second time. One doubts whether she is dead, for the ice appears to be made of painted white cardboard and the face that momentarily appears above the dark waters is not Garbo's face but that of a doll or a mannequin. This is as it should be, for her wild progress over the snow and ice has an oddly surrealist character, and we are not expected to believe in it. The Whore of Babylon has met the fate she deserved, the goddess has vanished, the commands of Pastor Voss have prevailed, and ordinary human beings continue to live their sublunary lives.

This should be the end of the film, but Hollywood has added its own commentary. In the last frames of the film, we see Gilbert doing exactly what life had always intended him to do. He is sitting at the feet of his old mother with his hands outstretched, holding a skein of white wool, while the light of Heaven falls on the old lady's hair. She smiles sweetly at him and he returns her smile. Hertha, the plain-looking childhood sweetheart, decides at last that she has had enough; it is time to leave, and she slips out of the house; a carriage with a top-hatted coachman is waiting for her. And so she goes out of history, while Gilbert as in a dream finds himself running after the carriage, the skein of wool still sticking to his hands, the plain-looking girl still smirking. And then, seeing that she is being followed by the man she desires most in the world, she leaps out of the carriage into his woolly hands.

Flesh and the Devil is a strange and troubling film, but not for any

reasons known to Clarence Brown or any of the actors. It has moments of high comedy, which were not conceived as comedy, and is never a tragedy. The excited flesh is visible only rarely and there is no real Devil. It shows the limitations of Garbo's acting, for there are scenes where her acting is totally inadequate, but it also shows aspects of her beauty that had never been seen before. The scene where she stands by the window and the reflected patterns of the rain ripple over her face is one example, and the astonishing flat, masklike face she shows during the love scene near the beginning of the film is another. William Daniels, who photographed her first American film, *The Torrent*, was beginning to learn how to light her face in such a way that it would appear to glow from within. He filmed the love scenes well but was careless with the rest. Yet, when he photographed her, he was becoming more certain of his craft, that craft which consisted of learning over a long period of time to convey all the subtleties of her face. He was learning lessons he would never forget.

The film was a commercial success largely because the public was fascinated by the love scenes, and was led to believe that a real love affair was taking place. The twenty-nine-year-old Gilbert and the twenty-one-year-old Garbo appeared to be perfectly matched. MGM distributed bulletins on the progress of the love affair to whet the public's appetite. Clarence Brown announced that he had never had an easier film to direct because the two principal actors were on fire with passion. "I am getting the best love scenes ever transferred onto celluloid," he declared. "I am working with raw material. They are in that blissful state of love that is so like a rosy cloud that they imagine themselves hidden behind it, as well as lost in it." No one seeing the film today would imagine they were violently in love; they appear to be close friends acting out a charade, unsure of themselves and a little perplexed by the demands made on them. The occasional incandescence of the love scenes derives as much from William Daniels' camera work as from the actors.

Many years later, when Gilbert was dead and his memory was fading, Garbo was asked about her romance with him. "There never was a romance," she answered, "and now I wonder what I ever saw in him."

The Gallant Lady

> This is the story of a gallant lady—
> a lady who was perhaps foolish and
> reckless beyond need—but withal
> a very gallant lady.
> —BESS MEREDITH

O<small>N</small> O<small>CTOBER</small> 6, 1927, at the Winter Garden Theater in New York, film, which had been blessedly silent for so long, burst into sound. The first words uttered on the sound track, spoken by Al Jolson in Coffee Dan's café in *The Jazz Singer*, were not altogether reassuring. They were "Wait a minute . . . Wait a minute. You ain't heard nothing yet." Henceforth the film was doomed to convey all the sounds heard on the set; every footstep would be recorded, and the squeaking of every door handle. In addition to the sounds heard on the set, there would be background music, manufactured to sustain the mood. Film became grand opera.

The puzzle is why sound took so long to come, for most of the problems connected with marrying sound to film had been solved by 1913. The small exhibitors did not want it; the large exhibitors were afraid of it; the studios were not prepared for it. No one doubted that it was coming, but there was a widespread hope that it would come later rather than sooner. Those who were most afraid of it were the actors who had untrained voices. MGM, which came late into sound films, possessed a stable of actors almost entirely without theatrical training. It had no

145

The Divine Woman

The Divine Woman, *with Lars Hanson*

voice teachers, no music department, and no plans even to experiment with sound. Irving Thalberg, the brilliant young director of productions, had stated publicly in the summer of 1927 that the talking motion picture would never replace the silent drama. So it happened that even after the introduction of the sound film, Garbo was able to make seven feature films—*Love, The Divine Woman, The Mysterious Lady, A Woman of Affairs, Wild Orchids, The Single Standard,* and *The Kiss* —in which no words were uttered and no background music was played except by the young lady at the piano who played snatches of the "Moonlight Sonata" during the love scenes.

MGM's blindness to the coming of sound was due largely to Irving Thalberg's belief that sound would destroy the illusions of silent film. He believed that titles conveyed emotions perfectly, and he had a high regard for the people who wrote them. He knew enough about the history of film to realize that the industry had developed techniques that would have to be changed abruptly with the coming of sound, and he was not prepared for the change, and had no conception of what it would entail. Singularly intelligent, he was also singularly obtuse. He announced that *The Jazz Singer* was a flash in the pan and the world would settle down to a continuous diet of silent films, for once people had heard sound they would soon grow bored with it. "Who," he asked, "wants to hear the actor's voice?"

The success of *The Jazz Singer* showed that everyone wanted to hear the actor's voice, whatever Thalberg's private opinion on the matter. Because he was a man who hated making compromises, it was only with great difficulty that he was induced to add a soundtrack to his next film, which was called *White Shadows in the South Seas,* starring Raquel Torres and Monty Blue. It was too late to add voices, but not too late to improvise a music score and to insert sound effects. The actors remained silent, but the seas were permitted to roar and the palm trees were permitted to rustle. In was an unsatisfactory compromise. Thalberg disliked the film, and he continued to make silent films. *White Shadows in the South Seas* was shown in New York in July 1928 without causing a single ripple of excitement.

Part of the trouble lay with politics. Louis B. Mayer, a confirmed Republican, was spending most of his time defending the cause of his friend Herbert Hoover, who was running for the presidency. He was on bad terms with Thalberg and on worse terms with William Fox, who succeeded in buying up a controlling interest in MGM and then lost it after being nearly killed in an automobile accident. Fox and Mayer were both totally unscrupulous, and they waged war without mercy. This monumental struggle had a lasting effect on the studio and especially on

Greta Garbo and Conrad Nagel

The Mysterious Lady, *with Conrad Nagel*

The Mysterious Lady, *with Gustav von Seyffertitz*

Thalberg, who suffered from a rheumatic heart, slept badly, and worked a fourteen-hour day.

Flesh and the Devil was a resounding financial success and Thalberg, following the long-established Hollywood practice, hoped to repeat the success with a very similar story. The difficulty was to find the right story. There were long delays and endless conferences. Finally he decided upon *Anna Karenina*, which he had never read. When he was able to read the novel, he learned to his horror that Anna throws herself under a train. He therefore gave orders that some more suitable fate must be found for her.

There was very little of the novel left when Frances Marion, the script writer, had finished with it. The adulteress, the lover, and the husband—Gilbert plays the lover and Brandon Hurst the singularly unattractive husband. Garbo, as usual, plays all the parts in the sense that she alone possesses any reality, and we see her husband and lover only through her reactions to them. Those wraithlike figures assume reality only through her presence. Once again, as in *Flesh and the Devil*, she demonstrates her unrivaled power to bring dead mutton to life. Her men become sheep, bleating their lives away.

It was not, of course, Garbo's fault. She had never been more radiant. There are close-ups in the film, which was finally called *Love*, as incandescent as any that came before or any that came afterward. They owed nothing to the nondescript screenplay and everything to the cameraman, William Daniels, who had fallen in love with her face from the moment he set eyes on it.

In the novel, Anna Karenina meets Count Vronsky in the most sedate circumstances, on a calm day, in Moscow, at the railroad station. In the film, Anna Karenina is being driven at great speed through a snowstorm on the road between Gatchina and St. Petersburg, and suddenly the troika comes to a stop because Vronsky has emerged from the snowy wastes and begs for a ride. Anna Karenina is heavily veiled as a protection against the storm. She is evidently a mysterious and important lady, and Vronsky is a raffish young officer who, when the troika reaches a village, prevails upon her to spend the night at the inn because the storm is increasing in intensity and the road will be blocked by snow and ice. It is not a very convincing argument, but for some reason it satisfies Anna. Slowly, at the inn, she removes her veil. Vronsky, like the audience, is immediately smitten. A snowstorm, Russia, a ravishing beauty, a long night of dalliance or perhaps of no dalliance at all. We know we are in Russia because the snow is piling up at the windows, the lamps are winking below the icons, and the gypsy musicians are playing. Such things will be arranged better in *Queen Christina*, when Gilbert meets Garbo

again in another country inn. In *Love*, he has no success at all, even though the innkeeper's wife amuses herself by placing Vronsky's luggage in Anna's room. He kisses her clumsily and is sent packing.

The scripts of Garbo's silent films tended to cannibalize each other; the same stock characters and the same stock situations reappear. Young officers, for example, appear on the parade ground and in the boudoir. The temptation to show them on the parade ground is almost irresistible. In the next scene we see Vronsky arriving late on the parade ground to be met by the long-suffering Grand Duke Michael, who commands his regiment, and the following conversation takes place:

> GRAND DUKE: What delayed you?
> VRONSKY: The storm.
> GRAND DUKE: Was she pretty?
> VRONSKY: Yes.
> GRAND DUKE: Blonde or brunette?
> VRONSKY: Brunette.
> GRAND DUKE: Any luck?
> VRONSKY: No, sir.
> GRAND DUKE: Go back to your place!

Vronsky thereupon returns to his place with a smirk of immense satisfaction. That night he encounters Anna again in the cathedral in St. Petersburg. It is Easter; total strangers are permitted to kiss one another; Vronsky takes advantage of the general license and kisses Anna on the cheek. She responds coldly. His suit has not been advanced; the husband is watching. Anna announces that she always takes candles home to her young son, and when we see her again, she is sitting by the boy's bedside; the passion she had failed to show to Vronsky is offered in a sublimated form to her son. She is very good at kissing little boys, and the love play around the bed becomes faintly embarrassing. Even more embarrassing is the sight of Anna praying before an icon, for she is far more beautiful than the Virgin.

Irving Thalberg had a large investment in John Gilbert, and he hoped that Gilbert would succeed in carrying his full weight in the drama. Special scenes were written for him, and Garbo was given clear instructions not to upstage him. She therefore held back, permitted him to upstage her, and smiled divinely whenever he overacted. Because he overacted most of the time, the audience was conscious only of the warmth and beauty of her smile.

It was not that Gilbert was an incompetent actor; it was merely that he was not credible, especially in close-up. He wears the white dress uniform of a Russian officer, which gives him definition and helps us to rec-

ognize him when he appears. The uniform, however, emphasizes his strutting walk and his curious inability to wear a uniform in a manner to suggest that he wears it habitually; it seems to be painted on him. His eyes roll, he gapes, he has perhaps the sickliest smile that ever appeared in films, and though he exhibited some ardor in the love scenes in *Flesh and the Devil*, he conveys no convincing ardor in *Love*. Garbo, too, is afflicted with a strange malaise, an occasional inability to act. There is a scene in which she sits with her husband in a box at the races. Vronsky is one of the riders, and she obviously hopes he will win. When his horse falls and he is thrown and perhaps badly hurt, Anna becomes hysterical, flings up her arms, rolls her head from side to side, and acts like a professional contortionist. It is the worst scene she ever played, and when Karenin tells her in the carriage as they drive home that he understands everything, we feel that she heartily deserves her fate—not for loving Vronsky but for putting on such a dreadfully inadequate display of hysteria, so wooden, monotonous, and ugly. Her fate, of course, is to be exiled from her St. Petersburg mansion and from her son.

The years pass. The lovers travel to Italy; Vronsky pines for the army; Anna pines for the son she has abandoned. From their appearance it would appear that the lovers cannot stand each other. When we return to St. Petersburg, we see Anna slipping into the Karenin mansion with a pile of presents for her son. She climbs the gigantic staircase, takes off her shoes, enters the boy's bedroom, and suddenly the screen is ablaze with an intense happiness as she plays with her son, showing off the presents, coaxing smiles from him, delighted to be home at last, dazzling the boy with her beauty and the strength of her affection, happier with him than she ever was with her lover. "I knew you would come on my birthday," the boy says. "They told me you were dead, but I never believed it." The toy monkey spins out of the box, the toy train speeds along the rails, Anna's face glows with an extraordinary light, and then a shadow falls across her face as Karenin enters the room. Once more she is exiled and abandoned. Vronsky is permitted to join the army only if he gives up his love affair, and so she lives obscurely, in loneliness and despair, until the time comes when Vronsky goes in search of her at the exact moment when she is contemplating suicide. She does not know that Karenin has died and the way is now open to her to marry Vronsky according to the rites of the church. At the end of the film they have found one another and are in each other's arms.

It is a strange ending for Anna Karenina but not altogether surprising, because almost no other ending would be permitted by the censors. The script writer has avoided the pitfalls of censorship only to plunge into the deeper pitfalls of absurdity. *Love* is a dime novel, but it is remem-

Wild Orchids

bered with affection because Garbo wandered through it in a kind of daze, sometimes smiling beatifically, coming vividly to life in the scenes with Philippe de Lacy, who was entirely credible and handsome enough to be her son; and always she retains her beauty and dignity. Too often the other actors seem to be scurrying around her like maddened homunculi, parading their carelessness and vulgarity, going through the motions of acting while they decide whether to go on acting; finally, having made the decision to act in her presence, they decide upon a charade, little knowing that she too, in her own way, has decided to act a charade, becoming a vamp, a destroyer of men, but not in the way intended by the script writer and the director. She has her own way of doing things and holds stubbornly to her own opinions of what the art of cinema is all about.

After *Love* she made six more silent films, all so much alike that scenes from one could be interspersed in another film without anyone being any the wiser. One of these films, *The Divine Woman*, is lost, for no prints survive, and it would not matter very much if the others were lost, for they contributed very little to the reputation of their directors. The most entertaining of the remaining five films is *The Mysterious Lady*, directed by Fred Niblo, with Conrad Nagel as the leading man and Gustav von Seyffertitz as the bearded arch-spy whom Garbo shoots dead to save the life of her lover. Happily, he falls into a well-uphol-stered chair, and when a servant enters the room, Garbo promptly sits on his knees, plants his hands on her lap, and pretends to be in the throes of a violent love scene. The servant tiptoes away, awed by the spectacle of Garbo radiantly ensconced on a Russian general's knees. Such felici-ties are not very frequent.

Conrad Nagel is a little less wooden than most of her lovers, and there are even moments when his features light up with intelligence. The opening scenes at the opera and a mysterious carriage ride at night hint at a closely knit spy drama, but the knitting comes unraveled after the Russian spy, Tania, and the German officer, Karl, have spent their first night together. Thereafter, with Von Seyffertitz in gold epaulettes and white uniform becoming increasingly suspicious of Tania's loyalty to the Russian cause, the protracted unraveling becomes a kind of hilarious game of stock situations and spectacular absurdities. "Karl, why have you come here?" Tania says. "Every moment you are facing death." Evidently death is a small price to pay for Tania's embraces. Conrad Nagel looks properly chastened, smiles weakly, thinks about death for all of two seconds, and decides to embrace her again. "We are made for each other," he says, and the statement goes unchallenged. Later the adorable spy will say without the least trace of suffering, "Karl, I had to

make you suffer, as I suffer." This is no longer a spy story; it is nine-teenth-century melodrama, full of good Germans in well-pressed uni-forms and bad Russians who drink too much. Tania only half believes she is a spy, and Karl has long since concluded that he is dreaming about a beautiful princess from Russia. Von Seyffertitz is the evil genie, and there must be some placatory offerings laid before him. His best line is "I taught you all you know, Tania, but I didn't teach you all I know." The best moment is when Tania most improbably jumps on his knees. *The Mysterious Lady* was not very mysterious.

Nor is *A Woman of Affairs* any better, though it is based on Michael Arlen's novel *The Green Hat*, which could have been made into an entertaining and honest film if the Hays Office had not regarded adul-tery with such extreme displeasure. Iris March is a happy adulteress, and the script writer, Bess Meredith, had somehow to suggest her extreme unhappiness. This was all the easier because the two lovers we are per-mitted to see at any length are Douglas Fairbanks, Jr., and John Gilbert. There is nothing to be said about either of them except that they act so incompetently that they become totally unbelievable and not even Garbo's enchantment brings any life to their wooden features. Gilbert is a caricature of a Latin lover, and Fairbanks plays the role of a well-bred young Englishman with altogether too much aplomb. He dies and makes a pretty corpse, and becomes interesting only when he is dead.

The novel maintains its excitement, for Iris March is a perfectly credi-ble figure, and Michael Arlen wrote about her with sympathy and at the same time with a kind of bewildered detachment. The opening words set the scene: "It has occurred to the writer to call this unimportant history 'The Green Hat' because a green hat was the first thing about her that he saw: as also it was, in a way, the last thing about her that he saw. It was bright green, of a sort of felt, and bravely worn: being, no doubt, one of those that women who have many hats affect 'pour le sport.'" Unfortunately the opening words of the film are less inviting. "This," wrote Bess Meredith, "is the story of a gallant lady—a lady who was perhaps foolish and reckless beyond need—but withal a very gallant lady." Poor, happy, syphilitic Iris March deserved a better fate. Clar-ence Brown, directing the film in his usual wooden way, followed the expurgated script with total fidelity, and the film comes to flickering life only when Garbo dies in a white hospital bed gravely ill, beautiful in her pallor and weariness, at peace with herself because Gilbert is standing beside her bed. For a moment her penetrating gaze breaks through the mists of illness and, surprisingly, she succeeds in seeing Gilbert as a man worthy of her adoration. "I'll get well now, if you won't leave me," she whispers.

Wild Orchids is more believable, perhaps because there was a new

A Woman of Affairs

The Single Standard, *with Nils Asther*

The Kiss

director, Sidney Franklin, and a more credible and appealing leading man, Nils Asther, who plays the part of a Javanese prince attempting more or less successfully to seduce Garbo from her avuncular husband, played by Lewis Stone. Franklin, confusing Java with Thailand, robed her in Thai costumes and a towering Thai headdress, thus offering a proper tribute to her beauty. Lewis Stone is stony-faced, and it is clear from the beginning that he is a husband in name only. Nils Asther is almost a credible lover. He possesses a natural elegance, and it is not impossible to believe that he is a Javanese prince. Even his palace, to which he invites Lewis Stone and Garbo, is almost credible. A tiger hunt, the dramatic highlight of the film, clearly takes place in California, not in Java, but the tiger commands our admiration if not our credulity. "The heat, the overwhelming heat strips everyone of pretense," the prince says in the torpor of a tropical night. One wishes it did. In the film Garbo returns to her avuncular husband. We, while watching the film, have reached a quite different conclusion. Garbo makes a commendable Oriental princess.

The Single Standard and *The Kiss* are mediocre triangle films remarkable only for the fact that the script writers seem to have lost their way in the scripts. Happily Nils Asther falls in love with Garbo in *The Single Standard*. Less happily, in *The Kiss*, Garbo finds herself involved with what appears to be a seventeen-year-old boy, a situation that is obviously unfair to the boy and can be regarded as cradle-snatching. Nils Asther, a Dane by birth, makes a credible prizefighter turned fashionable painter, and when he is alone with Garbo on his yacht, their Scandinavian temperaments are violently quickened. The scenes on the yacht are superb and deserve a better film.

In these absurd, broken-backed dramas with their improbable plots and impossible posturings, Garbo played her parts well. She was always quiveringly alive even when she was in the arms of a homunculus. She knew what she was doing. She was like a great dramatic actress reduced to working in the circus, learning the art of the bareback rider, the sword swallower, and the clown, until at last she could do all these things perfectly and almost without effort, yet all the time she was yearning to abandon the circus and enter the theatre.

Her face was now thinner, her eyes larger, her skin more luminous, her technique more resilient. She seemed to be preparing herself for a great dramatic role, but her employers convinced themselves that nothing more could be expected of her than the role of a vamp. But the days of silent films were now over, and so were the days of the vamp. Sound demanded an entirely new approach to filmmaking, and her employers sought anxiously for a subject that would permit her to speak.

The Fog-Bound Coasts

Fog, fog, fog, all bloody time. You
can't see where you vas going, no.
      —From *Anna Christie*

Wᴴᴱɴ ᴛᴏᴡᴀʀᴅ ᴛʜᴇ end of 1929 MGM decided to present Garbo in a sound film ("GARBO SPEAKS"), they turned to Eugene O'Neill's play *Anna Christie*, which had the advantage that two of the main characters, Christopher Christopherson and his daughter, known as Anna Christie, would speak with formidable Swedish accents. It was an obvious choice. Unfortunately, like many obvious choices, it was the wrong one. *Anna Christie* is a complex and difficult play that suffers from some of Eugene O'Neill's worst writing. The main character was originally Christopher Christopherson; after much reworking, the playwright attempted to shift the focus to the daughter and to let the father act as a chorus. What was originally a character study of an old, embittered seaman became a study of an even more embittered twenty-year-old prostitute.

Eugene O'Neill was profoundly dissatisfied with his play. He had good reason to be, for the various parts do not fit together, the sentimentality of Anna's Irish lover is thicker than Irish fog, and there is, as always in an O'Neill play, far too much talk and too little action. This meant that Garbo would have a good deal of talking to do, and for what

167

appeared to be many hours, the characters would be bogged down in incessant self-questioning. The prostitute, the father, and the huge, muscle-bound, semi-literate lover who finds it maddeningly difficult to justify his love for an admitted sinner, hold the stage. The rest of the characters are mere spear carriers.

O'Neill, who had begun by calling the play *Chris Christopherson*, came in the end to the conclusion that he should have called it *Comma* because it was no more than a small incident in an unwritten play. This was an avowal of failure, but for the wrong reason. O'Neill succeeded brilliantly in saying what he wanted to say, but unfortunately he said it too often, and very often in the same words. The vigor of the play comes from the father and the daughter, their almost incestuous relationship, the perfect understanding they have for one another. George Jean Nathan objected strongly to the happy ending, for Anna finally makes her peace with her Irishman, but O'Neill rightly pointed out that it is only relatively happy, for they are at the mercy of absolute and terrible forces. "Fog, fog, fog, all bloody time," says Chris in the famous closing words of the play. "You can't see where you vas going, no. Only that old davil, sea—she knows!"

So there is Anna Christie, aged twenty, recently released from a prison hospital, sick and morbid, terrified by men, penniless and helpless, and there is her father, who is busily drinking himself to death, having come to the end of his long affair with the fat and shabby wharf rat Marthy Owen, who has comforted him as best she could. She wears a man's cap, a double-breasted jacket, and a grimy calico shirt; she has a red nose, and the veins are breaking all over her face; and her stringy gray hair is piled up like a bedraggled nest. Marthy Owen is a real character, and as played by Marie Dressler she is as memorable as Garbo. It was not really fair to put Garbo in a film with Marie Dressler: perfect beauty encountering perfect humanity. Unhappily the script writer abandoned Marie Dressler very early. From time to time the unhappy spectator yearns for her to come back and put life into a dying thing.

In the past Garbo in her American films was pitted against actors and actresses who had not a fraction of her talent. Confronted by Marie Dressler, for whom she possessed a genuine affection, Garbo was at a disadvantage. There was never a moment when Garbo was a convincing prostitute who had worked in a house in St. Paul, and there was never a moment when Marie Dressler did not resemble to perfection a fat and hilarious wharf rat. "Her breath comes in wheezy gasps," read the stage directions. "She speaks in a loud, mannish voice, punctuated by explosions of hoarse laughter. But there twinkles in her bloodshot blue eyes a youthful lust for life which hard usage had failed to stifle." That was

Anna Christie

Anna Christie, *with Marie Dressler*

Marie Dressler to the life! The description of Anna Christie by Eugene O'Neill suggests that there might be difficulties in casting Garbo for the part. He wrote, "She is a tall, blond, fully developed girl of twenty, handsome after a large, Viking-daughter fashion but now run down in health and plainly showing all the outward evidences of belonging to the world's oldest profession. Her youthful face is already hard and cynical beneath its layer of make-up." Here was the problem, for Garbo was no large Viking daughter and she could portray hardness and cynicism only with the greatest difficulty. Above all, it was impossible to imagine her as a twenty-year-old prostitute.

Nevertheless she plays the role with great intelligence, and there are moments when she is almost convincing. The first scene is the best. She enters the saloon, pale and worn out by a day and a half's train journey, sits down heavily at the table where Marie Dressler presides like an earth goddess, and says in a voice that sounds strangely familiar, "Gimme a whisky wit yinger ale on the side, and don't be stingy, ba-bee!" It is an electric moment, for the audience has been waiting for five years to hear her speak, and at last she has spoken. The words are intelligible. They tell us that she is a heavy drinker, and from this we deduce that she has had many misfortunes in her life, and we find ourselves at once sympathizing with her. Unhappily for the theatrical illusion she looks uncommonly like Garbo and is all the more beautiful because she wears plain, dark clothes and a cloche hat that never hides her face.

"GARBO SPEAKS" read the advertisements, as though this were a matter for surprise. In fact, she spoke in a deep, throaty contralto that was attractive and beguiling but not always intelligible, because she sometimes swallowed her vowels and always maintained her Swedish speech rhythms. Indeed, the film suffers from a terrible plethora of accents. George F. Marion, who plays her father, looks like a Dutchman and speaks a language deliberately contrived to sound like a foreigner speaking English, and does it too well, so that it always seems to be contrived. Charles Bickford, who plays a shipwrecked sailor washed up onto Chris Christopherson's hospitable barge, speaks with a mechanical Irish brogue. All the actors are so busy with their accents that they ruin the free flow of words.

Bickford, playing Mat Burke, a stoker from an ill-fated steamer, is a study in imbecility. An original hairy ape, he thumps his chest and pronounces that no woman has ever made a fool of him and that any woman he sets eyes on must immediately surrender to his charms. He squeezes Garbo's hand to make a point, and very nearly breaks it. " 'Tis a clumsy ape I am. It's a great power I have in my hand and arm, and I do be forgetting it at times." He forgets tirelessly. By overacting and having nothing to say, although he is constantly talking, Bickford very nearly succeeds in ruining the film. It is not his fault. Eugene O'Neill has given him very little leeway. Mat Burke is presented as the ape with a conscience, the indefatigable grand inquisitor. He makes Anna Christie swear on a crucifix that he is the only man she ever felt love for, and realizes too late that she is a Lutheran and therefore not bound by an oath. On this curious note the play comes to an end: the oath, which may be broken, and the deceptive sea.

Inevitably the sea becomes equated with sex: they are both to be enjoyed, to be propitiated, to be feared. In the stage production, the sea is never seen and is all the more menacing because it is invisible. In the film it is occasionally visible and seems harmless, with the result that Chris Christopherson's weightiest comments on it seem oddly inappropriate. No attempt has been made to render the sea imaginatively, perhaps for the same reason that no attempt has been made to construct a believable barge. The inexpensive set we see on the screen is a small cabin with an oilcloth table top, some cupboards, and a door. Sometimes, when the director remembers it, a cabin lamp will swing with the motion of the waves. The cabin itself never acquires verisimilitude. It is obviously anchored on a sound stage and is very far from the sea.

Such things are disturbing, for they make Garbo's task all the more difficult. As the prostitute trying to reform, trying to claw her way back into her father's affections, trying to live sensibly and quietly on the barge, trying to forget, trying to survive, she needs all the assistance she can get to be convincing, and neither the film setting nor her improbable father nor her unlikely shipwrecked sailor is of much help to her. The illusion must come from her. Once more, as so often in the past, the full weight of the film falls on her shoulders.

It might have been better if Frances Marion had kept closer to O'Neill's play and had not written new scenes to take place on the waterfront and at the fun fair in order, as she wrote, "to give the picture movement away from the confines of a dilapidated old tub tied up at the pier." In her view a well-rounded film must have a lot of comedy; she provided it in abundance, though it had little enough to do with the story and nothing in common with O'Neill's style. Her chief contribution to the film was to insist that Marie Dressler should play Marthy, and Irving Thalberg's chief contribution was to permit Frances Marion to write her own version of the play, which is considerably less entertaining than the original. Hollywood had not yet learned that great dramatists should do their own rewriting. A flawed play with a still more flawed screen adaptation continually breaking at the seams was the vehicle for Garbo's first appearance on a sound stage.

Greta Garbo and George F. Marion

Garbo at first detested the play because it depicted Swedes as poor, down-at-heel vagabonds, rootless, hating the sea that gives them their livelihood, small-minded, bitter, and sodden with drink. She was reminded that Christopher Christopherson and his daughter were American citizens: the film had nothing to do with Sweden. When Frances Marion wondered aloud whether Garbo would tear up her contract and return to Stockholm, Thalberg had a quietly cynical answer. "She won't," he said. "The Beverly Hills bank where she kept her savings went under in the crash."

It was the time when the bread lines were beginning to form and the soup kitchens were opening all over America. But the film industry was still vigorous, though beginning to reflect the anxieties of the age. Already there were films showing the hard, black, metallic underside of life, the knife-thrust of poverty, and there would be many more. Soon there would come the films of poverty-stricken horror and the musicals with the resounding titles *Ten Cents a Dance* and *Brother, Can You Spare a Dime?* Even in *Anna Christie* there were hints of the Depression which was beginning to engulf the world.

As Thalberg predicted, Garbo accepted the role assigned to her. She came to her first rehearsal in good spirits, and if she still had reservations about the subject matter of the film, she succeeded in concealing them. She said, "I have learned my lines, Mr. Brown, and I am ready to rehearse." Nervous and shy, she generally showed little animation on the first day of rehearsal, but it was remembered that she was unusually cordial to the other actors. Later, as the film progressed, her reservations about it were revived. Some of her worst acting occurs during the mawkish love scenes with Charles Bickford at the end of the film, when she is plainly tired and confused. The last ten minutes of the film are singularly wooden and unappetizing.

Clarence Brown was not exactly a man of infinite resources. He liked to set up the camera at a considerable distance from the actors; he expected the actors to know their lines; he followed the script. He had the property owner's love for solid and substantial things, and he liked heavy furniture, cigars, ships, land, houses. His films show little understanding of the intricacies of the human mind and the wayward riches of human personality. He was not happy in the make-believe world of Hollywood, and as soon as possible he retired to look after his extensive properties.

A rather unimaginative director has, however, certain advantages. Given a brilliant script, he can and sometimes does give an accurate rendering of it. The trouble with *Anna Christie* lay in the script. Occasionally Frances Marion incorporated scenes as O'Neill had written them, and these were sometimes rendered with quite extraordinary power because they were accurately and prosaically recorded by his camera. One suspects that he would have done better if he had been given a real saloon bar and a real barge.

Thus, in the opening scenes in Johnny-the-Priest's saloon, near South Street in New York, we are introduced into a world that is reassuringly solid, familiar, and even respectable. Almost we can believe that George F. Marion is Christopher Christopherson. In the play he is short, chunky, wide-mouthed, with a drooping yellow mustache and a thick neck "jammed like a post into the heavy trunk of his body." Gradually, as the film progresses, we come to realize that it is precisely that neck like a post that is lacking. He is a strong man in the play, but in the film he is a weak and garrulous man continually whining about "that old davil sea." Impossible to believe that he was ever the lover of old, fat, decaying Marthy! Marie Dressler, all two hundred pounds of her, would not waste herself on this shrimp of a seaman. Like Garbo she aspires to grandeur; she enters the saloon bar like a drunken Empress. She is wonderfully endowed with humanity, and no richer, riper character ever graced the screen. So it happened that in *Anna Christie* two empresses encountered each other over a table top, one disguised as a burly New York slut with a laugh like the roar of a steam engine, the other disguised as an embittered, white-faced prostitute from St. Paul with a croaking, whining voice. No one has had any difficulty penetrating these disguises.

Marie Dressler was a profound student of drama and an inordinate hell-raiser. Her private life was grotesquely unhappy, but on the stage and on the screen she exuded a volcanic good humor. She studied Garbo closely and came to some intelligent conclusions. "Garbo is lonely," she said. "She always has been and always will be. She lives in the core of a vast, aching loneliness. She is a great artist, but it is both her supreme glory and her supreme tragedy that art is to her the only reality. The figures of living men and women, the events of everyday existence, move about her, shadowy, insubstantial. It is only when she breathes the breath of life into a part, clothes with her own flesh and blood the concept of a playwright, that she herself is fully aware, fully alive."

Marie Dressler always spoke and acted with authority, and her interpretation of Garbo is therefore more authoritative than most. She was able to study Garbo at close quarters without falling in love with her or being blinded by her beauty.

Clarence Brown directed four more films with Garbo. They were *Romance, Inspiration, Anna Karenina* and *Conquest*. In all of them he was strangely heavy-handed, and his hobnailed boots can be heard striding across the sound stage. It is not an entirely infelicitous sound and is sometimes more interesting than the conversations on the screen.

The Fog-Bound Coasts

Romance, like the ill-fated *Two-faced Woman*, is one of those films that cry out for an extenuating cause. It was originally written by Edward Sheldon as a three-act stage play and was one of those dramas that defy transformation into film. A young man tells his pipe-smoking grandfather, who wears the full uniform of a bishop, that he is about to marry an actress. The bishop demurs. He, too, was once in love with an actress, or rather with a prima donna. It was a long and wrenching love affair complicated by the fact that the prima donna was already the mistress of the prodigiously wealthy Cornelius Van Tuyl. In flashback, the bishop, then the young rector of St. Giles, wins her away from the millionaire only to discover that he is in love with her for all the wrong reasons—he wants only her flesh, not her soul. She resorts to prayer, to save him, and then vanishes out of his life, leaving him a wiser and better man. Most of the film consists of a lengthy recapitulation of a love affair that could be told in three minutes.

Happily Bishop Armstrong, played by Gavin Gordon, and Cornelius Van Tuyl, played by the venerable Lewis Stone, consistently act in the same elegiac key and, by being interchangeable, cancel each other out. Both claim to be the prima donna's protectors, talk about their great love for her, fondle her, desire her, and resemble the aspidistras, glossy, odorless, and completely without significance, that decorate the Van Tuyl town house. When she asks the young rector about St. Giles, he answers promptly that he has the honor of serving one of the most important saints of the English church. She is amused and fascinated by his innocence, his hangdog adoration, even his puritanism, for he does not drink, has never attended the opera, and has quite evidently never been in love with a woman. Gavin Gordon does his best to convey enthusiastic innocence, as later he does his best to convey the hopeless lusts of the flesh: his eyes roll, his neck jerks within the confines of his clerical collar, his nostrils dilate fiercely; he employs the methods of the silent screen to convince himself that he is in love.

Margherita Cavallini, the object of his affections, moves calmly and serenely through his passions like a knife. She draws blood with every glance, and if she half opens her lips he becomes her slave for ever. She is perfectly aware that she is fanning the flames, and at the moment when the rector reaches the "brink of life and death," she withdraws from the combat with a whispered "Thank you for having loved me." Garbo makes even these words intelligible. She can even hold a lock of his baby hair to her cheek and whisper, "Oh, it is so soft," and for a moment we believe the emotion is genuine. She can put on his mother's necklace and make us feel that this is somehow a sacramental act. It is only when she sits down at the piano and plays for him that we begin to wonder why

Romance

she has blundered into this *mésalliance*, which is obviously doing him no good, for at the piano she is sufficiently separated from him to be observed as a person in her own right. At such moments her lover mercifully escapes into the surrounding shadows, and when he appears again we are compelled to ask ourselves who he is. Garbo's lovers are so easily forgotten.

As Margherita Cavallini, the famous prima donna, Garbo is never quite convincing, but there is never a moment when we are allowed to forget the famous beauty, the forever unattainable woman of the world. She wears her fabulously expensive furs as though she were a Russian princess, and she is in her element when she rides along snow-covered Fifth Avenue in a sleigh. Hollywood had at last made the discovery that she looked most beautiful against the snow, and having made this discovery it promptly forgot it. In *Queen Christina* and *Anna Karenina* the enchanting snow maiden would be allowed to return briefly.

After *Romance* came three more disastrous films before *Grand Hotel* provided Garbo with the opportunity to deliver a bravura performance as the famous ballet dancer Grusinskaya, whose career is coming to an end and whose hopes of happiness rest on her love for a middle-aged scoundrel, Baron von Gaigern, who dies most inopportunely and heroically.

The three films were disastrous in different ways; in all of them, as in *Romance*, Garbo is asked to commit the supreme act of renunciation. To save a man she will leave him or sacrifice her life, and the fact that the man is totally unworthy of her is the least of her preoccupations. Implicit in the philosophy of Hollywood was the knowledge that a woman reached her highest fruition at the moment when she renounced all that made her a woman. It was a philosophy derived from the sentimental novels of the nineteenth century, and it had the advantage of presenting her with the opportunity for several dramatic crises. She takes and eats the apple, rejoices in its poison, permits herself some reasonable doubts, offers the remains of the apple to Adam, retracts the offer, and finally assumes the whole burden of the guilt, allowing Adam to go scot-free. In this grotesque mythology Adam has all the advantages.

In *Inspiration* Garbo plays Yvonne, an artist's model in Paris with a murky past, who is loved by a rising young diplomat, Robert Montgomery. She finally leaves him to save his career, but not before she has gone through many of those crises described by the rector of St. Giles as "standing on the brink of life and death." Love, it appears, is terribly dangerous. People commit suicide out of love. Yvonne's friend Liane throws herself out of a window when her lover rejects her, and Yvonne is made all the more aware of her responsibilities. The film was based,

Greta Garbo and Gavin Gordon

without acknowledgment, on Alphonse Daudet's novel *Sapho*, published in 1884. If the film had followed the novel more closely, it might have been worth making. Daudet was a remarkable novelist with a penetrating psychological understanding of his characters. Here is a fragment that suggests the flavor of the work:

"On the third floor above the entresol, the most convenient place in the world for throwing oneself out of the window!"
As she spoke the young woman smiled, red-cheeked and luminous in the fading light, her heavy bunch of purple flowers in her hand; and the tone of her voice was so deep, so solemn, that no one replied. The wind freshened; the houses opposite seemed taller.

Something of this mood is captured by Garbo as she wanders wide-eyed through Gene Markey's travesty of Daudet's novel. Sometimes she appears to be looking over her shoulder in the hope that someone will tell her what the film is all about, and at other times she appears to be lost in her own meditations, which have nothing to do with the film. Robert Montgomery conveys exactly the right insipidity demanded of a young diplomat, and Garbo's conversation with him is as insipid as his character. "I am just a nice young woman," she says wistfully, "not too young and not too nice." At the end, sitting by the fire, she writes a letter telling him to marry the rich girl, and without a moan or a sigh she steals away into the dawn.

Susan Lenox: Her Fall and Rise, directed by Robert Z. Leonard, with the young Clark Gable as Garbo's leading man, is more adventurous. It asks us to believe that Garbo is a wild, barefoot farm girl in imminent danger of being given to a man she detests. "Helga, you're going to marry Ed Mondstrum," she is told by the father who sired her out of wedlock. Shrieks, whistling of whips, scurries in the bedroom, until she escapes through an enchanted forest to the lonely dog-guarded house of Clark Gable, who pretends to be surprised to find her in his garage. It is love at first or second sight. Garbo, surprisingly, shows herself to be a good homemaker for the lonely bachelor and attends to his creature comforts with cautious enthusiasm. "Who are you, anyway?" he asks her, after giving her a pair of pajamas. It is a question many people have asked, and we are no nearer a solution when we see her in those improbable pajamas.

The role of her father is played by the genial, avuncular Jean Hersholt, now provided with three days' growth of beard and a terrible temper. He goes in search of her, finds her, and is about to take her home and force her into marriage with Ed Mondstrum when she escapes

on a carnival train. Here, for a few moments, Garbo is in her element among the circus folk. It is astonishing how easily she fits into Burlingham's Carnival Show. The tattooed lady, the painted clowns, the circus horses, and the merry-go-rounds provide her with exactly the atmosphere where she is most at ease. But Clark Gable is still pursuing her, and soon she is on the run again. When we next see her, she is a rich man's doll in New York, amusing herself in a penthouse with a sinister roulette wheel. Here Clark Gable finds her, and she announces her undying love for him, only to be rejected. Then the tables are turned, and instead of being pursued, she becomes the pursuer, catching up at last with Clark Gable in a sleazy dance hall in Puerto Sacate, where, broken in spirit, looking like a Bowery bum, he works and drinks his life away in a construction gang. Meanwhile Garbo has become the mistress of another rich man, who owns a yacht and offers her a life of ease, promising to sail away with her to Arabia and Egypt. The prospect is not especially inviting, and she makes her great act of renunciation, spending the remainder of her days with the Bowery bum.

Susan Lenox: Her Fall and Rise, based on the popular novel by David Graham Phillips, makes very few demands on the spectator. We see Garbo in a large variety of costumes against many backgrounds, and in some she looks careworn and in others ethereal, according to her mood. But mostly she has the appearance of a somnambulist who speaks like a ventriloquist's dummy. For the first time we discover that we are sorry for her—sorry because the director is unable to tell a coherent story and because she is clearly unfitted for the role of a high-grade prostitute, passing through the arms of a succession of improbable men. And at the same time we are pleasurably excited to see her in so many settings, even if those settings are simply plaster and tar paper extravaganzas on the MGM lot. She has been released from the boudoir into a prostitute's cage in Puerto Sacate, and who knows? We may find her in Tahiti or Hongkong or even acting in a Nō play in Kyoto.

Alas, in her next film she is taken to an imaginary Paris during World War I, and she is no more credible as the spy Mata Hari than as the barefoot peasant girl who rises in society to play roulette in a New York penthouse. Incredulity is awakened from the moment we see her dancing, nearly naked, wearing a few bits and pieces of Oriental costume, in front of a grotesque carving of the Chinese god of war, who will appear again with suitable embellishments in *The Painted Veil*. She addresses the many-armed god: "I dance for you tonight, as in the temples of Java." She does not dance. Instead, she makes a few schoolboyish wriggles before lurching off the stage to resume her career as a spy for the Germans, in particular for a certain Adriani, played by the inscrutable

Susan Lenox, with Clark Gable

Lewis Stone wearing a goatee, whose ostensible occupation is that of a keeper of a gambling saloon. Ramon Novarro, with his effeminate Spanish good looks, is cast as a valorous Russian officer who falls into her clutches. She does in fact clutch him vigorously, while the Madonna lamps wink beneath the Icon of the Virgin of Kazan and the portrait of Tsar Nicholas II gazes impassively from the wall. The Russian atmosphere is poured on like hot borscht, and we might be in St. Petersburg. Novarro possesses secrets; it is her business to find them, and Adriani is always impatient. Carlotta, another beautiful spy in his network, fails to produce the goods and is murdered horribly by a club-footed man who appears out of nowhere. The film is in danger of becoming a horror movie rather than a spy thriller. Novarro, blinded in an airplane accident, is brought at last to the prison where Mata Hari lives out her last hours, having been arrested by the French authorities with the greatest of ease. The days when Adriani can say, "You are sailing for Amsterdam tonight; report to H12" are now over. She seems to have no regrets. With her head shaved, wearing a black gown, she descends the steps from her cell after bidding a calm farewell to her former lover, and the execution squad marches her off. Garbo goes to her death quietly, with the poise of an Empress about to be beheaded.

The public had no reason to be grateful to the script writers, Benjamin Glazer and Leo Birinski, who cluttered up the story with far too many red herrings and far too much stilted dialogue. "One day," Mata Hari warns her lover, "you may know that I am something less than the woman you think me." It is a plain warning, but the hapless Russian officer is in no mood for warnings. When he comes to her in her prison cell, he is told that he is entering a sanatorium, and Mata Hari explains that she too is about to be operated on, "but the operation is not a dangerous one." She renounces her lover and her life in almost the same breath. The nuns in their starched white hoods move protectively around her in the discreet silence reserved for moments of dedication and sacrifice. Suddenly she is on a stairway, majestically alone, more beautiful than at any other moment in the film, and soon, instead of the nuns, she is surrounded by poilus with long bayonets. That descent in slow time is the only pure cinematographic passage in the entire film. Then at last, in silence, without benefit of script writers, Garbo redeems all the infantile errors of the film and provides us one of her most sharply memorable scenes. Long after we have forgotten every conspiratorial incident and every kiss, we remember the door opening at the top of the stairs.

The trouble with *Mata Hari* is that the script writers forgot the real Mata Hari, who was considerably more interesting than the cliché-

ridden character they invented. Half Dutch, half Javanese, she was born Gertrud Margarete Zelle in what was then the Dutch East Indies. Although not beautiful, she could make herself up to be beautiful, and she had grace of movement and a lean, sinewy dancer's body. She settled in Paris before World War I, and was known for her love affairs, her well-tailored clothes, and her habit of riding every morning in the Bois de Boulogne, wearing the top hat and the flying veil of an earlier age. Count Robert de Montesquieu, who became Proust's Baron de Charlus, was one of her admirers, chiefly because she resembled a boy. Once, dancing nude before an audience of aristocratic women, she suddenly realized that one member of the audience was a man in disguise. She was dancing a war dance, wielding a spear, and nearly ran him through. When the war came, she proved to be one of the very best spies in the German apparatus by acquiring lovers high up in the French Ministry of War. She was completely immoral, ruthless, and dedicated. Arrested, she maintained her calm, and when she was taken out to face the firing squad at Vincennes, she wore a well-tailored suit, walked with firm steps, and shouted *Vive l'Allemagne!* in the few moments left to her before a young French lieutenant raised his sword and gave the order to fire. She was a complex, courageous, and uncompromising spy, and deserved better than to become the subject of titillating articles in the Sunday supplements.

Garbo, playing a real spy, might have made a film more memorable than any she had made up to this time. Instead, she made a film that is memorable only for a single scene at the very end.

Romance, Inspiration, Susan Lenox, and *Mata Hari* were all failures. They added nothing to her stature, made a great deal of money, kept her name before the public, and were quickly forgotten. Quite suddenly the years of fumbling came to an end with *Grand Hotel,* when she stepped into a part that fitted her perfectly. The film is kitsch, the script is shoddily written, most of the actors overplay their parts, but Garbo's performance is breathtaking in its lightness and grace. She plays Grusinskaya, the nervous and aging ballerina, as if she were eighteen years old. She has the wrong shape for a ballerina. It does not matter. She invests the role with magic, convinces us that she is indeed Grusinskaya, and then goes on to convince us that she is capable of falling in love out of loneliness and desperation with a common thief who slips into her room to steal her jewels. It is absurd that we should care, but we do care. Once more the actress has triumphed over her material. She is eighteen years old, she is an aging ballerina, she is Garbo, she is not and never will be a dancer, she seems to walk with ten-foot strides across the lobby of the Grand Hotel, and none of this is important. What matters is that she has caught the essential character of the ballerina, becomes it, lives it. There is no gesture, no turn of the face, no intonation that is not wholly in character. Garbo vanishes, and Grusinskaya comes to life.

This time the bravura performance is such that it no longer has the appearance of being one. She delights in being capricious, and Grusinskaya is nothing if not capricious. She delights in the beauty appropriate to a ballerina, and shows it to perfection. She delights, too, in adventure and finds it most implausibly in entertaining her gentleman thief, Felix Benvenuto Freiherr von Gaigern, played without any distinction at all by John Barrymore. Inevitably he becomes "Flix." It is a suitable name for that seedy and aging lecher, who preys on women who are well provided with jewelry. "Flix" is as close to being nonexistent as most of her screen lovers, and he owes whatever reality he possesses to her protecting influence. He becomes real because we want him to be so, because it is inconceivable that this astonishingly beautiful ballerina should not have a lover. In the same way she protects all the others who act close to her: her manager, her lady's maid, her chauffeur, even the desk clerks when she passes them on her way in or out of the hotel.

The scenario by William A. Drake, based on Vicki Baum's novel, is scarcely to be believed. All the stock characters are present: the good-hearted secretary, the tough, flint-eyed businessman, the sad, desiccated employee having his last fling at the sumptuous hotel, threats of bankruptcy, commercial empires toppling, murder at night. There are scenes, such as the murder, that possess a kind of stale effrontery. Is it possible, is it to be believed, that after all these years of cinematographic murders there should be a murder contrived so inexpertly, so obviously? So, too, when the rich industrialist Preysing faces ruin, we have to witness his business enemies and creditors sitting around a table while he tells lies to them, attempts to stave off disaster, and goes into paroxysms of rage when he is reduced to the same level as his former employee Kringelein. The board meeting is hilarious chiefly because it resembles so closely a meeting of studio executives. It has been pushed into the film by main force for no reason that anyone can now discover. Preysing's descent into hell is a thing to wonder at, for no one ever descended quite so woodenly, with the body going thump-thump-thump down the invisible stairs.

The English director, Edmund Goulding, possessed two valuable characteristics: a feeling for place and an understanding of women. If he could not quite make a believable secretary out of Joan Crawford, he could invest her with enough dignity to make her into a believable woman. He was less successful with the men. Lewis Stone, playing a long-time habitué of the hotel notable for the livid scar that destroys half

his face, a brooding monster who somewhat resembles the monsters who stand guard outside Chinese temples, from time to time announces philosophically that people come and go, and nothing ever happens. He has a useful place in the film as the official moralist. No one pays the slightest attention to him. He is a mask periodically making the noises appropriate to despair. Unfortunately, having been introduced as a gimmick, he is entirely uninteresting.

Sir Cedric Hardwicke, a brilliant actor and admirable critic, said that Goulding made several errors that, given his opportunities and the number of highly paid actors in the film, are inexcusable. "Goulding," he said, "had completely overlooked the dramatic possibilities of the story and used it merely as a series of exercises for the stars." There is some truth in this, and there would be more if the actors had really performed their roles intelligently. Most of them overacted; none, not even the suave Freiherr von Gaigern, was convincing. Nor were they helped by the script, which is particularly deadly when spoken by the men. "I shall die on the gallows," the Freiherr announces imperturbably. He is clearly aiming too high, since it is indisputable that he will eventually go to jail. The lines given to Garbo are not much better. "I can't dance tonight," the ballerina says mournfully. "Everything is cold and finished, so far away, so threadbare. The Russians, St. Petersburg, the Grand Duke Sergey . . . Sergey dead . . . " She is lamenting the distant past, for the Grand Duke Sergey was assassinated by the poet Ivan Kaliayev in 1905. We have entered a timeless world; the Grand Hotel is outside of time, and Garbo-Grusinskaya is timeless. She attempts to commit suicide with veronal, but the gentleman thief saves her "just in time." The hotel room is reached by John Barrymore with the greatest of ease, for we are permitted to see him climbing along a ledge that is obviously no more than six inches off the ground. He goes through the motions of teetering forty stories above the street, but of course there is no street, no forty stories, no latch on the window. He enters the ballerina's room with the dignity of a man who is accustomed to marching into boudoirs.

In spite of the batteries of telephone girls, in spite of the vast, circular hotel, in spite of the desk clerks, the elevator operators, and scar-faced Lewis Stone periodically reminding us, like a Greek chorus, about the vanity of life and of hotel life in particular, we are never quite convinced of the reality of the Grand Hotel. But of the reality of the twenty-six-year-old aging ballerina we have not the slightest doubt. She glows like the full moon with a blinding beauty, and is never more beautiful than when, bidding farewell to the world, wearing her white ballet costume, she removes her shoes and kisses them, and moves around the room touching and saluting the objects she will never see again after she

As You Desire Me, with Erich von Stroheim

has taken veronal. Out of this scene there will come, in *Queen Christina*, the scene where she moves around another bedroom, touching and caressing the objects she encounters with quiet fervor, worshiping and adoring.

The magic of *Grand Hotel* is provided by Garbo alone. Suddenly it became clear—or should have become clear—that she had been entirely wasted in roles where she played the vamp, the *femme fatale*, the seductress. Her reach was as high as she wanted to go. The Greek tragedies, Shakespeare, and Chekhov were waiting for her. Instead, they put her into a senseless melodrama based at a remote distance on Pirandello's play *As You Desire Me*. Gene Markey wrote the script, Hedda Hopper played Garbo's sister, Erich von Stroheim loved her, and Melvyn Douglas thought she was his wife, but was not quite sure, for she suffered from amnesia and was uncertain of her own identity. Was she Zara, the Budapest cabaret singer, or the Countess Varelli? It was a matter that could be decided by an intelligent investigator in five minutes, but Gene Markey was able to spin it out for seventy-one minutes. Everyone acted atrociously. Erich von Stroheim succeeded in caricaturing himself, and in addition he forgot his lines. "I never knew at any moment what I was supposed to be doing," Melvyn Douglas has said. "It was beyond the understanding of any of us." This, of course, was the intention of Pirandello, but in a different sense. "There is nothing left in me, nothing of me," Zara–Countess Varelli says. "Take me, take me, and make me as you desire me." But whatever protean shape she assumes, she is scarcely desirable. Garbo has finally achieved the impossible. She is no longer beautiful. Instead, she is pasty-faced, a wooden stick wearing a white wig. It is as though all the actors resented the story and George Fitzmaurice's direction, and went on strike.

Paul Bern, who produced the film for MGM, later committed suicide standing stark naked before a mirror in his palatial house on Benedict Canyon. He left a note to his wife, Jean Harlow: "Dearest dear, Unfortunately this is the only way to make good the frightful wrong I have done you, and to wipe out my abject humiliation. You understand that last night was only a comedy. Paul."

The strange thing about Hollywood was that it had no sense of tragedy. Its lifeblood was drama, but it had not developed a sense of drama. It had no set of values, did not know where it was going, and did not care. It drifted with the tide. There were too many Paul Berns who thought everything was comedy and the easiest solution was to kill oneself. *As You Desire Me* was an irretrievable disaster: the ship sunk without a trace, and threatened to sink everyone connected with it.

Queen Christina

I am not a mirage, Antonio.
                        —From *Queen Christina*

OVER THE YEARS the legend of Garbo had been growing, but it was a disturbing legend with very little except her beauty to support it. If she had died in the summer of 1932, when her contract with MGM came to an end, she would have been remembered as an accomplished actress who played brilliantly in a number of films without ever coming to her full stature. Some of these films, like *Romance* and *As You Desire Me*, were disasters. *Anna Christie* showed that she could act creditably in films for which she was totally unsuited. With the single exception of *Grand Hotel*, where she was given an intellectually credible and satisfying role, she was usually compelled to act against the grain in stories that were unworthy of her, that were no more than five-finger exercises and made no great demands on her. In Hollywood it was accepted that she was a vamp, the successor to Nazimova, Theda Bara, and Pola Negri, and she must therefore be given roles in which she could exhibit a certain resourcefulness in bringing men to their doom. It was a satisfying formula, but it had no relation to her abilities. When she was very young, in *Gösta Berlings Saga* and *The Street of Sorrows*, she showed an extraordinary ability to sustain a rich and complex role, and in all the

201

Queen Christina by Sébastien Bourdon

years since then she was never asked to play a role half as difficult or half as rewarding. She had not advanced in her craft; she was continually retreating.

For years the stories she played in were trivial. She acted with grace, ingenuity, and vitality, and she had only to appear on the screen for the audience to become totally oblivious of anyone else. She commanded attention. In her presence all others became shadows, but no one quite knew why she commanded so much attention or why the others were blotted out. The real actress was rarely permitted to emerge. There were brief glimpses of her, but there were never enough of them. Even when the stories were absurd, her mere presence on the screen was enough to give dignity to absurdity. Yet those brief glimpses of her, when she gave the appearance of acting at the very height of her powers, suggested that she was capable of sustained effort. She resembled one of those high mountains that are seen dimly and momentarily through the mist. Days and months pass; the mountain remains obstinately concealed; then one day the mist and the clouds roll away, and there is the white mountain superb against the dark indigo sky.

She knew she was being wasted and complained bitterly about her roles. There was scarcely any part she could not play on condition that it had a grandeur commensurate with her beauty and ability. One could imagine her in *Othello, Antony and Cleopatra,* or *The Cherry Orchard,* or indeed in any of the great heroic dramas. She could be Medea or Iphigenia, Empress or courtesan, madcap or clown, but she could not continue to be simply the adventuress, the temptress, the mysterious lady. *Mata Hari* had shown the dangers of Sunday-supplement stories for so accomplished an actress. Only at the very end, when she walked down the shabby stairway to the execution ground, had there been a hint of what she could accomplish as a tragic actress. She had walked through the rest of the film as though in a daze.

The face of Garbo during the last moments of *Mata Hari* belonged to a new order of refinement. As she grew older, her face was being chiseled into hitherto unknown forms. She was still recognizably Garbo, but it was Garbo with experience, with knowledge of the world, and yet not completely belonging to the world. There was something goddesslike in that calm and serene gaze. So Athene must have looked when she first gazed upon the Greek landscape after issuing from the head of Zeus.

Toward the end of his life, John Keats wrote a poem called "Hyperion: A Vision" in which he described the appearance of a mysterious goddess called Moneta. When the poet comes upon her, she is majestically enthroned high up in the mountains of the soul; she is veiled and the smoke of a censer helps to obscure her appearance. At last, in answer

to his prayer, she removes the veil and for the first time he is able to see her as she is:

> *Then saw I a wan face,*
> *Not pin'd by human sorrows, but bright-blanch'd*
> *By an immortal sickness which kills not;*
> *It works a constant change, which happy death*
> *Can put no end to; deathwards progressing*
> *To no death was that visage; it had past*
> *The lily and the snow; and beyond these*
> *I must not think now, though I saw that face.*
> *But for her eyes I should have fled away;*
> *They held me back with a benignant light,*
> *Soft, mitigated by divinest lids*
> *Half-clos'd, and visionless entire they seem'd*
> *Of all external things; they saw me not,*
> *But in blank splendour beam'd like the mild moon,*
> *Who comforts those she sees not, who knows not*
> *What eyes are upward cast.*

Such, then, was Garbo as age smoothed out her features and gave them an astonishing refinement. The face of Garbo seen in close-up is like the face that Keats saw in a poetic vision—so austere, so benignant, so far removed from all temporal and extraneous characteristics. She was never more like a vision than when the camera drew very close to her. By the alchemy of cinema, which transformed flesh into light, she acquired an almost unearthly beauty and an exquisite radiance. Even Hollywood was beginning to see that she was being totally wasted.

Perhaps it is in the nature of things that this waste, almost amounting to the loss of a great talent, should have taken place. Hollywood was a somnabulist's paradise. It did not know what it was doing, and the system of rule by committee and script writing by teams of script writers was doomed to produce banality. An extraordinary art form, the sound film, had been placed in the hands of Philistines, and they scarcely knew what to do with it. Garbo had made fifteen films in America, and out of all these she could legitimately be proud of perhaps ten minutes of *Flesh and the Devil*, a quarter of an hour of *Anna Christie*, twenty-five minutes of *Grand Hotel*, and a single minute of *Mata Hari*. The rest of her films were the purest kitsch. They were made memorable only by her presence, and no one was particularly concerned about what she did, whom she loved, what fate overcame her in the end. It was enough simply to gaze at her face; the story had no value.

Today when we attend revivals of *Romance, Inspiration, Susan Lenox,* and *As You Desire Me*, it is with the feeling that we are entering the dark and gruesome Middle Ages. We see impossible stories told in an impossible manner by actors who still gesture awkwardly as they did in the silent films. The lighting is haphazard. The sets have obviously been put together with floorboards, tar paper, and string and then painted over. The direction is uncertain, and the camerawork is usually shoddy. What is missing is precisely what is most necessary: excitement, the probing of personality, conflict. Hollywood succeeded in vulgarizing even the best stories, reducing them to a common level of mediocrity. D. W. Griffith alone was able to take a story and fill it with abundant life and conflict and probe deep into the personalities of his characters. He was the only director of genius produced by Hollywood and had no successors.

Garbo had been trained by Stiller, who showed in *Sir Arne's Treasure* that he too possessed the authentic fire of genius, and she was becoming increasingly exasperated by the quality of her film roles. She had long been a star of the first magnitude, but this star was in danger of drifting out of the heavens altogether. She felt it was time to make a film that would be worthy of her. She was an avid reader of history, especially Swedish history, and had long felt a great sympathy for Queen Christina of Sweden.

The Queen was a bluestocking who spoke French, German, Italian, and Spanish and read Latin and Greek with remarkable fluency. She was undersized and had a long, narrow face with thick lips, drooping eyelids, a powerful pointed nose. She suffered all her life from depressions, fainting spells, abscesses, and heavy colds. She dressed like a man, swore like a man, and hunted like a man. "There is nothing feminine about her except her sex," wrote Father Mannerschied, the priest of the Spanish Ambassador. "Her voice, her manner of speaking, her walk, her style, her ways are all quite masculine." This was not quite true. She had a woman's rages, a woman's jealousies. She enjoyed the flattery of her admirers and was especially pleased when she was complimented for her intelligence. Her continual studies made her nearsighted, and she could not recognize people unless they were very close to her. Her father, King Gustavus Adolphus, was killed at the battle of Lützen when she was six years old, with the result that she was brought up in an atmosphere of court intrigues and proved to be the best intriguer of all. She was his only child, the heir to the throne, and well aware of her power. Like many lonely, fatherless children, she was very complex, moody, and assertive, and given to terrible temper tantrums. On December 8, 1644, her eighteenth birthday, she took the oath as King of Sweden. Her correct title was therefore King, not Queen, Christina.

With Elizabeth Young

Small, ugly, with one shoulder higher than the other—a consequence of being dropped by a nurse when she was very young—Christina nevertheless possessed great spiritual beauty. Everyone who encountered her remarked on the wonderful way her face lit up when she was excited. Her charm, when she chose to display it, was excessive. She possessed the imperial manner and an imperial graciousness, and could be very subtle in granting favors. She was reputed to have many lovers but in fact had none, her only sentimental attachment being to Ebba Sparre, one of the court ladies. She was a lesbian in an age when lesbians were very rare. She was King of Sweden, and no one was permitted to forget it, yet in March 1654, when she was twenty-seven years old, she abruptly abdicated and spent most of the remaining years of her life in Rome, where she collected books and paintings and intrigued with cardinals and popes. As she grew older, she grew fatter, more calculating, more peremptory, and continued to exert her power and her charm. She died quite suddenly at the age of sixty-three, saying that she wanted on her tombstone only the words: VIXIT CHRISTINA, which may be translated: "Christina was someone who once lived." She never revealed why she abdicated, and it appears likely that she found the exercise of power wearisome and absurd, feeling that she had better things to do with her life.

The film *Queen Christina* has very little to do with the historical Christina. It could more properly be called *Variations on the Theme of Queen Christina*. As such its script is wonderfully imaginative and intelligent, for it succeeds in capturing the essence of Christina's madcap youth, her delight in dressing up as a boy, her intolerance, her charm, and her waywardness. Garbo herself was devoted to the subject, took part in the writing of it, and quite naturally acted as the chief authority on Swedish history. Of all the films she made, this is the one she likes most, and for good reason, because it contains much of her best acting. At last she was permitted to act in a film worthy of her.

Queen Christina and *Camille*, which she made three years later, were her supreme achievements in America. In these films there is never a moment of faltering. She completely dominates the screen and is seen almost continually, and when she is not seen, we are aware of her invisible presence. In both roles she plays a queenly figure, at once dignified and maddeningly impetuous, and in both she is doomed.

The story, as finally written on the basis of some scattered facts and many surmises, inevitably involves a battle for the affections of the Queen. The contenders are Charles Augustus, the Prince Palatine, who was her cousin; Count Magnus de la Gardie, whose father was a member of the Regency Council; and Don Antonio Pimentel, the Spanish

Ambassador. Charles Augustus was fat and slow-moving, and would have made a bad husband and a worse lover. Count Magnus, who belonged to a French family long settled in Sweden, was gentle and charming; it was widely rumored that he was the natural son of Gustavus Adolphus and therefore her half-brother. Don Antonio was also a man of great charm and sophistication, and the scriptwriters properly gave him the role of chief contender while changing his name from Pimentel to de la Prada, perhaps because it was easier to pronounce.

The game played by the script writers was to extract the utmost excitement from the pursuit of the Queen by three men. This was perfectly legitimate, as in fact at least eight men at various times believed they were in love with her, while she herself wrote that she was in love with none of them. Queen Christina was not an infallible witness to the truth, and there is very little doubt that she was a notorious flirt, while her deepest affection went out to Ebba Sparre, her lady in waiting. Sexually precocious, but withdrawn and attracted to both sexes, Christina enjoyed the best of both worlds.

The high point in the film is the portrayal of her first meeting with Don Antonio at an inn during a snowstorm. This scene derives directly from the opening scene of *Love*, which was an abysmal failure. This failure is now transformed in the most improbable way into an extraordinarily successful evocation of the sudden flaring up of a love affair. Christina, dressed as a boy, finds herself sharing a room at the inn with the youthful ambassador. She is nervous, excited, and too radiantly beautiful in her boy's attire to be completely convincing. She would prefer to spend the night sitting by the fire; the ambassador would prefer to spend the night in bed with her. Exactly how and where they spend the night is never clearly explained, nor is an explanation necessary. The snow falls; they are its prisoners and must wait until the storm subsides and the road to Stockholm can be opened.

Some attempt is made to convey the raucous atmosphere of the snowbound inn, with roaring boys serving the hot grog known as *glopp* and with serving wenches up to their usual mischief. The low, smoke-blackened beams echo with quarrels and wild laughter. A vast number of rowdy people have evidently taken shelter from the storm. There is a sense of bustle, violent movement; knives flash, private wars are declared, and then quite suddenly and unexpectedly the boy Christina and Don Antonio are in a large, elegantly furnished room, and there is between them one of those long and happy silences that are the first fruits of affection. We do not ask ourselves how they could possibly rent so palatial a room for themselves, especially in an inn that caters to soldiers and their wenches. Why such a large room? Why is it so quiet? Why are they in what appears to be a bedchamber in a palace? The truth, of course, is that the film is imposing its own laws on the imagination. The room is vast because the imagination needs the space, because Christina needs room, because the very vastness of the room has something to say about their love affair. Don Antonio does not know he is confronted by the Queen, and the Queen does not know he is an ambassador, though it can be assumed that he is a Spanish nobleman, a grandee, perhaps one of those foreign knights who take service under the Swedish crown.

One morning Christina wakes up wearing a very unboyish nightgown. She wanders around the bedroom like someone in a trance, touching and caressing things—the hangings, the furniture, a bowl of large, juicy grapes. She is either sleepwalking or engaged in a dream of the purest happiness. She seems to be floating around the room, bemused, bewitched, joyful, smiling the secret smile of the blessed. What she is in fact attempting to do is to fix in her memory every detail of this room, which has given her so much happiness, or at least this is the explanation she offers Don Antonio when he asks her what she is doing. She answers, "I am remembering this room." The answer tells us no more than we knew already. Meanwhile the amazing slow dance continues as she recites all those things she wants to store in her memory against the time when Don Antonio will be separated from her.

This dance is one of the most magical things ever created in Hollywood. It has very little to do with the story and nothing to do with Christina as Queen of Sweden. It is an interlude, a gift, an evocation of the joy of being in love, and it seems to have sprung spontaneously out of the mind and soul of Garbo. In fact, it was carefully choreographed by Rouben Mamoulian, the director, who said later with only slight exaggeration, "It was done to a metronome." He explained to her, "This has to be sheer poetry and feeling, like a dance." As she dances dreamily around the room, she suggests an intensity of happiness that is almost unbearable. There is no longer a veil between the audience and the actress; she has become the dancer and the dance.

Hollywood, which owed its existence to the happy discovery that almost any love story could be transformed into film, rarely portrayed lovers imaginatively. At the end of the film the lovers would fall into each other's arms and there was a convenient fade-out. The long-established formula was strictly adhered to, for the film was intended to depict the trials and struggles of young lovers, not the fruition of their love. It was believed that the audience would be titillated and excited by the lovers' efforts to come closer to one another, but the embrace would be reserved for the last frames. What happened after the embrace was

left to the imagination of the audience. The formula exacted the utmost sense of frustration, and the audience paid for the privilege of watching and sharing the frustrations of the principal actor and actress.

But as Garbo wanders ecstatically around the bedchamber, murmuring, "I am remembering this room," she is celebrating her perfect joy, her delight in love and the world and everything in it. Film, like music, can express the utmost joy and the deepest misery, yet it rarely attempts to do either of these things. This time film is used with exquisite art to do something that must have seemed almost impossible, and is all the more moving, all the more enchanting, because Garbo, alone among actresses, could express the very height of happiness without moving a muscle of her face. She had only to dance around the room and everything had been said. No words, no music were necessary. The magical ability of film to express emotions nakedly was vindicated. Sound, which had never been essential, was seen to be wholly extraneous.

So it happens sometimes that some passages in a sound film appear all the more vivid when the sound is turned off. The nobility of Paul Muni's face in *Pasteur* is breathtaking; it has all the lineaments that one imagines might mark the visage of a great doctor; he immersed himself in the part, studied medicine, read every available book on Pasteur, invented business with his hands and a curious way of nodding his head that we feel instinctively to be absolutely right if we are to have an imaginative reconstruction of this great doctor and humanitarian; but when he opens his mouth the script writers make him say things that no French doctor would ever dream of saying. The film distorts Pasteur's life to a degree that is almost unbelievable. Incidents were invented to make Pasteur more combative and more heroic. Napoleon III becomes an enemy of Pasteur; his courtiers are depicted as nonentities concerned only with stamping out Pasteur's discoveries; and at the very end of the film, after a lifetime of battling against the authorities, the Institut de France summons him and begs his pardon for all the errors that have been made by officialdom. But it did not happen like this at all. Imaginative fiction may change incidents, but it may not distort them. A true image of Pasteur emerges only when we see Paul Muni in his laboratory or in the commonplace events of his daily life. When he is fitted into a plot, he vanishes. Nevertheless the mask, the light on his face, the feelings expressed by his eyes wonderfully convey the essence of Pasteur. Muni, silent, achieves what he fails to do when he opens his mouth.

Something very similar happened with Garbo. Her silences spoke louder than her words, which were often unnecessary, for she could express herself vividly with the faintest inclination of her head, the gentlest of smiles, or the slightest movement of her eyes. She was an amazing

mime, and her very beauty made her miming more effective. She says to her Spanish lover, "I am not a mirage, Antonio." The words merely say something he, and we, knew before. When she stalks across the bedroom, embracing one by one the bedposts, the bolster, the table top, and a bowl of grapes, we do not want to hear her lover say, "What are you doing?" Yet this is what he says, the words having been supplied by S. N. Behrman, who should have known better. Like Paul Muni, Garbo was forced to say things that were better left unsaid.

Sometimes, too, she is compelled to say things that have more to do with her own legend than with Queen Christina. When she said, "I think marriage is an altogether shocking thing. How is it possible to think of a man sleeping in the same room?" the script writer is being archly clever by weaving Garbo's known abhorrence of marriage into the texture of the film. "I shall die a bachelor," says Queen Christina, who has stolen the words from Garbo. "Your Majesty, would you be an old maid?" Lewis Stone asks her, and we listen much more intently because we know that Garbo has willingly considered such a fate. This stealing from Garbo to illuminate Christina partakes of cannibalism; we forget that Christina also illuminates Garbo.

Perhaps it was inevitable that the roles of Garbo and Christina should have become confused, for Garbo herself was an Empress. She had the dignity and reserve of an Empress, and the appalling loneliness. The temptation to use Garbo to explain Christina appears to have been irresistible.

S. N. Behrman took a philosophical attitude toward the script. Literal accuracy was abandoned; an imaginary Queen Christina was invented; the studio executives demanded at least three love scenes, of which one must be demonstrably incandescent. Behrman explained his method cautiously, while emphasizing his indifference to history:

> We took a background of historical fact, and worked out our characterizations and emotional interactions from that point. I think that taking so-called dramatic liberties with a historical script is a very natural and inescapable process. In the case of Christina, so little is known about the Queen's private affairs and personal biases that the picture is probably as close an approximation of the facts as anything could be. The main point at issue, of course, is: Does the characterization emerge as a warm, living, human being? If this is answered in the affirmative, your historical play has succeeded.

If Behrman is not entirely convincing, it is because the studio executives were riding herd on him. He was rewriting the script daily under great pressure: John Gilbert, who plays Don Antonio with the *élan* of an elephant, was constantly reporting sick (he was drinking heavily to fortify himself for his confrontations with Garbo), and the executives were complaining bitterly about the cost of the film, which they would never have undertaken but for Garbo's insistence. As a result the script is curiously inconsequential, events follow one another without logic, the fatal duel between Count Magnus and the Spanish nobleman is never sufficiently explained, and even Queen Christina's decision to abandon the throne is introduced quite arbitrarily and unconvincingly. Nevertheless the film, like assorted jewels strung together, possesses a disorderly splendor. Queen Christina lives, and while nothing around her lives with the same intensity and much of the film resembles a shadow play, we are grateful for the presence of that slender, imperial figure who convinces us that she is a Queen.

The variations on the theme of Queen Christina were extemporized, changed direction from day to day, and were all the more lively and enchanting because the development of the story was haphazard, like history. The ceremonial life of the court was properly emphasized, the Queen was provided with a suitably dignified treasurer and chamberlain in C. Aubrey Smith, and Lewis Stone, looking even more British than usual, was the Chancellor Oxenstjerna, the real power behind the throne. Kingly dignity was maintained. Garbo did not look ridiculous sitting on a throne. On the contrary she looked more queenly than any Queen.

Cedric Gibbons, the perennial art director, searched for the actual throne Christina had sat in and made a replica. He also searched for her globe. This proved more difficult, because it had left Sweden long ago. He finally found it in the Huntington Library in Pasadena, fifteen miles from the MGM studios. Although Rouben Mamoulian gave careful instructions that the costumes should be the simplest possible so that the actors would not feel constrained, an elaborate wardrobe deriving from various centuries was devised and Don Antonio was outfitted according to the court costumes painted by Velazquez. None of this matters very much, but a huge painting of King Gustavus Adolphus riding on his charger has the appearance of being painted by a Hollywood amateur artist and seems out of place. Neither Garbo nor Christina needed these props, and the film might have been even better without these distractions, or if it had been played in modern costume.

The studio executives were anxious to obtain favorable impressions from historians and took special care that the palace in Stockholm should be accurately rendered on the set. Because the palace was reputed to be very old, a man with a paint box and lampblack was ordered to go around the palace set every day to make sure there would be visible evidence of old age. He painted fresh cobwebs and candle drippings and ensured that the painted cracks in the plaster and tar paper remained visible. No one in the audience was aware of them, and it was all wasted effort.

Garbo held the strings in her hand. This time she was determined that the film should be free of those tensions that come about as a result of miscasting. MGM wanted Laurence Olivier to play the role of Don Antonio. She objected firmly. Olivier was given a screen test, acted a love scene with her, and was confronted by a woman so ice cold that it became immediately evident that she could not, and would not, act with him. He was hurt and puzzled, wondering what he had done to offend her. He had not offended her. He was simply not the actor she had envisioned for Don Antonio. She chose John Gilbert because he looked the part. That he had once been in love with her and was now evidently losing the last vestiges of his popularity apparently did not concern her, nor was she in the least impressed by the fact that he was perhaps the heaviest drinker in a hard-drinking city. She liked him but did not love him. Years later when she was asked why she showed him so much affection while filming *Flesh and the Devil*, she answered, "I was lonely —and I couldn't speak English."

Gilbert did everything that was demanded of him. In a career given over to a succession of intolerable performances with the single exception of the American soldier in *The Big Parade*, he was intolerable to the very end. He was scarcely visible in *Queen Christina*. He postured, said the words he was ordered to say, and looked so little like a Spanish grandee that he could have been taken for an American gunman, his dark clothes being vaguely reminiscent of the gunman's black leather costume. Like so many people in Garbo's films, he appeared to have wandered onto the set by accident and seemed to be looking for an excuse to go home. He had nothing to say except that he loved her, and he said it without conviction. He died of acute alcoholic poisoning some months later, on January 9, 1936.

The real hero of the film was Rouben Mamoulian, who had the good sense to let Garbo play the Queen in her own way. He was sensitive to her moods, understood her need for privacy, asked her none of those perplexing and irritating questions that were always being asked of her, and was devoted to her first as an actress and only secondarily as a woman. Inevitably he fell in love with her, and just as inevitably the brief love affair came to an abrupt end. But while they were making the film, he acted as her artistic conscience, arguing, as Stiller had done, about the precise way in which a scene should be played, the exact gesture, the exact inclination of the head, and doing this not so much as a director but as a friend, a very close friend. In this way he succeeded in entering her mind and reinforcing her own interpretations. Thus, for the very last scene, when she is on shipboard and leaving Sweden for ever, having abandoned her whole past life for an unknown and unpredictable future, he suggested that at this moment she should not show any expression at all, but instead leave her mind an utter blank and look as impassive as possible. This she did, but it should be observed that this was originally her own idea. As we shall see, something very similar occurs at the end of *Anna Karenina*. But where in *Anna Karenina* her impassive features suggest total defeat, in *Queen Christina* they suggest a heroic victory over herself.

There is nothing in the least heroic about her next film, *The Painted Veil*, based on a story by William Somerset Maugham and directed by Richard Boleslawski. This is one of those free-falling disasters that were the commonplace of Garbo's film career. In theory, a play set against a Chinese background with Garbo in the leading part should have been wonderfully successful. Garbo as a Chinese woman would have been perfectly credible, and the landscape of China would have provided the perfect setting for her beauty. China, so mysterious and so bloody, with the Japanese armies already on the march, had innumerable stories to tell. MGM chose to portray her in the dullest, most mechanical story of all.

In *The Painted Veil* Garbo is a bored English housewife married to an overworked doctor in China. To escape from boredom she has an affair with a British diplomat played by George Brent. He is an unlikely lover, and her husband, played by Herbert Marshall, is an unlikely husband. To punish her, the doctor insists that she accompany him to a hospital in the plague-ridden interior, where she is more bored than ever. Happily, a few moments before she is about to die of boredom, her husband is stabbed by a Chinese who objects to his order to burn down the town in order to save it from the plague. This gives her something to do, and she nurses him back to life, wearing her crisp, white nurse's uniform with an exquisite propriety. She looks serene and lovely, but she has nothing to do except to smile and brood over him and change his bandages. Herbert Marshall and George Brent do a vanishing trick, and we are aware only of Garbo moving incongruously through a landscape that has little resemblance to China.

In the eighteenth century there arose a debased form of Chinese design that came to be known as *chinoiserie*. In *The Painted Veil*, *chinoiserie* is let loose. We see pagodas totally unlike Chinese pagodas, cross bridges that have never existed in China, and attend ceremonies such as might be invented by a drunken nightclub owner after seeing the New Year ushered in in San Francisco's Chinatown. We are treated to an

The Painted Veil

enormous temple on a hillside, an enormous stairway, an enormous golden dragon, enormous numbers of beautiful Chinese dancing girls. The Chinese god of fate is to pronounce judgment. He is grim-faced, which is proper in a god of fate, but his methods are capricious. The dancing girls and the dragon vanish amid flames; the judgment is pronounced; the nightclub routine is revived. A travesty of Chinese ritual is followed by a travesty of a soured love affair. "I don't love you. I never did," she tells her husband, who is excited by the prospect of journeying to Mei Tan Fu, three hundred miles away in the interior. She seeks comfort in the arms of the vice-consul. His arms fail to comfort her because his mind is elsewhere; he cannot take her as a wife or mistress without jeopardizing his career. So she returns to her long-suffering and limping husband and is carried by sedan chair across the interminable Chinese countryside, which looks suspiciously like the countryside of southern California. And when at last they come to Mei Tan Fu, the first dead are being carried out of the town. "Why am I here?" she asks dazedly, and her husband answers bitterly, "You are here because Townsend would not have you at the price." The statement may be true. "Why am I here?" is uttered with the full heart. Garbo has not the faintest idea what she is doing in the film and moves through it like a sleepwalker.

She speaks some words in an unknown dialect of Chinese, wears the latest Paris fashions, and looks fetching in white silk. She plays her scenes in a low key, for there is nothing to be high-keyed about. Indeed the music is so low that it finally becomes inaudible. It is a film to go to sleep by.

Clearly many things have gone wrong: the story, the scene, the plot, the characterization, the direction, the choice of actors, the design of Garbo's clothes, and the photographs used in back-projection. There seems to have been a conspiracy to reduce Garbo to meaninglessness. Cool, beautiful, austere, her pale face suggesting the perfection of purity, she resembles Kuan Yin, the Chinese goddess of mercy, but otherwise has no connection with China.

MGM was forced to do some hard thinking. No longer could they afford to put her in Somerset Maugham stories. They thought so well that her next two films were to be counted among her acknowledged masterpieces.

Anna Karenina

Beauty has the strange power of
prolonging all emotions—even the
emotion of terror.
                —VAL LEWTON

ONE DAY IN the late summer of 1950 the producer Val Lewton, the
creator of many low-budget films that became minor classics, drove with
me to a drive-in movie on the outskirts of Hollywood. He was a handsome man with a rather heavy Russian face, glowing eyes, thick curly
hair, and a manner of great sweetness and gentleness. He had somehow
survived the neurotic wars that interminably flared up in the studios;
he had even survived betrayal by two of his most cherished protégés;
and if on this particular evening he was sad, it was a natural sadness such
as a man might feel after a long day's work in the studio. It was evening,
there was thunder in the air, and we went to the drive-in cinema showing
a Betty Hutton musical because, as he said, "You can learn something
from any goddam, stupid film and sometimes you can learn very important things from the very stupidest films."

So for about half an hour we watched the film, and then, because it
was excruciatingly boring, he turned off the sound and began to talk
about his own films and the problems he had encountered in Hollywood. The screen blazed with color and movement, and from the neighboring speakers we heard the faint crackling of the sound track. He was
talking well, but there was something oddly valedictory in his words, as

though he did not expect to say them again. He had grown heavier during the last few months. Within six months he would be dead of a heart attack.

"I don't know why I was always fascinated by the terrible," he said. "When I was a child, I lived in a world of my own, full of ghosts and monsters and scaly things. I would look up and see an army of the most frightful green snakes swimming in the sky. They were the branches of a tree, and I knew they would come down and swallow me, and that they were snakes, and that they were absolutely pitiless. And then my mother would call to me and I would go into the house for lunch as though nothing whatsoever had happened. But all this was pretense. My real life consisted of contemplating more or less cold-bloodedly, more or less courageously, the absolutely terrible things that happened all around me.

"All this, I suppose, was useful when I began to make low-budget horror films for RKO. I knew a great deal about horror, because I have always been horrified. I knew in particular that very ordinary things have the power to convey the utmost horror—the branches of a tree, a knot in wood, a gap in a fence, a stone lying on a path. There are certain kinds of stones that demand to be thrown and to kill. There are cracks in wood which lead to the most terrifying kingdoms. I am not talking about death but about terror, which quickens life. Shadows, too. There are shadows that can make a man cry out for mercy.

"I felt very strongly that film was always a shadow play. I thought it would be possible to build up a horror story out of shadows. Imagine a room where a man is quietly reading a book. His wife has gone out to see a movie, a cat is curled up at his feet, his pipe lies on a low table beside him. It is the most ordinary scene imaginable. Suddenly a shadow appears on the wall—a shapeless shadow in which the audience can imagine anything it pleases. Gradually they realize it is the shadow of a panther moving very stealthily toward the man who is reading. The shadow springs. The man lifts his hand to ward off the panther's paws. The lamp is knocked down. It is almost dark. We imagine we see in detail exactly what is going on. The panther has struck at the man's throat, it is clawing him, tearing him apart. The audience is terrified because it has been given the freedom to terrify itself, having seen nothing and imagined everything. Then we see a hand groping for the lamp which has fallen, and we discover that nothing has happened except that the cat jumped up on the table and overturned the lamp, and the audience sighs with relief. But the next time they will not sigh with relief, because we can so arrange the shadows that they will be more real and more menacing. We can construct a world of shadows, each one more menacing than the one that has gone before.

"In the film *Cat People* we never see a black panther except when the heroine visits a caged panther in the Central Park Zoo. But at intervals during the film we see the shadow of a panther; it is always approaching; it is always present. The audience sees the shadow even when it is not there. There is a sequence in an indoor swimming pool. The girl is swimming, and nothing could be more ordinary, more leisurely. But then comes the panther's shadow and the sound of its breathing echoing across the swimming pool, and there is a crescendo of terror. That commonplace swimming pool, to our surprise, generated more horror in the audience than any other scene. Probably we should not have been surprised. The spaciousness, the ordinariness, the openness of the swimming pool—and then of course it was the last place in the world where you would expect to see a black panther.

"It was during the making of this film that we discovered something that was totally unexpected. We wanted to maintain the atmosphere of terror as the heroine makes her way across a long balcony, thinking she is being pursued by the panther. It was a long-drawn-out scene, deliberately so. Quite by accident we had placed a table with an enormous bowl of flowers midway across the balcony. We realized later that the enormous bowl of flowers had solved the problem, for the audience, seeing it in all its beauty, was momentarily distracted but only half distracted, and the flowers served as a vehicle to sustain and carry forward all other emotions. We discovered that a beautiful face or a beautiful sculpture or a painting or a beautiful landscape accomplished the same purpose. We learned that beauty has the strange power of prolonging all emotions—even the emotion of terror."

Val Lewton professed to being a little surprised by this discovery. The strange thing was that the beautiful object need not have anything to do with the story: a Chinese painting or a Chinese sculpture would have served as well. He explored this effect at some length in his later films, most notably in *Bedlam*, set in the Hospital of St. Mary of Bethlehem in eighteenth-century London. It appeared to be an invariable rule that beauty sustained all emotions. A solitary object, chosen almost at random, the only condition being that it must be breathtakingly beautiful and that the audience must have time to absorb its beauty, could be inserted into the scene to prolong and sustain it and even to heighten it.

All theories about film agreed that emotion is carried by the movement of the film, that the motion picture differs from most other art forms because it is relentlessly and continuously in motion. But the bowl of flowers was not in motion; the camera paused in front of them; they were quite still; and emotion flowed through them, being sustained by their beauty.

Val Lewton's theory of the sustaining power of beauty throws some light on Garbo's role in cinema. Those memorable close-ups resemble the bowl of flowers: They are beautiful in their own right and have very little to do with the unfolding of the story. Garbo's beauty sustains the improbable story, makes it appear probable, gives dimension to something that has no dimension, and makes the intolerable tolerable. She is the one real thing on the screen, and her reality endows all the unreality around her with shape and form.

At one time Val Lewton had thought of writing an aesthetic of the cinema, an inquiry into the mysterious things that can be accomplished in cinema and in no other art. But he was too practical and too improvident to carry out a theoretical discussion at any length. In that long monologue in the drive-in cinema he seemed to be attempting to sketch an aesthetic based on his own experience.

Although the discovery of the bowl of flowers phenomenon took place in 1942, something very similar occurred seven years earlier in the making of *Anna Karenina*. He was at that time a production assistant to David Selznick, who was deeply concerned about finding a suitable ending for the film. There would be shots of the train, the smoke, the wheels, the pistons. Garbo's face would be seen through the smoke, the train lights would flicker on it, there would be rising music to convey her emotions, and then quite suddenly there would be the smoke drifting away, and silence. Her suicide under the wheels of the train would become all the more real if it was imagined and not seen by the audience. All this had been agreed upon by the producer, the director and the script writers. But how to accomplish it? It was Val Lewton who suggested that it was not at all necessary to photograph Garbo continuously as she stood by the railroad track: all that was necessary was to take a single frame and repeat it. She looks very somber. Gusts of smoke pour across her face. The audience sees the conflicting emotions written on her face and the sudden resolution that finally led her to throw herself under the wheels, but in fact it was seeing only what it imagined. What was actually thrown onto the screen was a still portrait of her chosen from among a thousand others. There was no change of expression, no flicker of an eyelid, no slightest movement of the lips or eyes. By a supreme invention of the cinema she was fixed in the rigidity of death before she died. Her invisible death on the screen was all the more heartbreaking, all the more inevitable, because it had been accomplished by using a single frame.

Anna Karenina was one of the very few Garbo films where there is an authentic note of menace throughout, and this comes about because we know she is doomed. (Mata Hari was also doomed, but the story was so

Anna Karenina, *with Maureen O'Sullivan*

improbable that we are deprived of any real sense of doom.) The film therefore made extraordinary demands on the script writers—Clemence Dane, Salka Viertel, and S. N. Behrman—who were determined to write a memorable film worthy of Garbo and, if possible, worthy of Tolstoy. Doom is conveyed in many ways—the many shots of railroad trains, wintry shadows, oppressive stairways, the separateness and loneliness of Anna Karenina, which can be emphasized by the camera and which are in any case implicit in Garbo's playing of the role. The subjects of the screenplay are the doomed woman and the working out of her doom, and the film therefore rightly concentrates on her love affairs and not on those of Kitty Oblonsky, which are scarcely less important in the original novel. Above all, it was intended to be Garbo's play, a bravura performance, with the supporting actors obtruding as little as possible.

As so often happened in Garbo's films, the supporting actors were, with a few exceptions, poorly chosen. Fredric March, who played Vronsky, Anna's lover, was peculiarly ill-fitted for the role, for there was nothing in him that could conceivably have attracted Anna. He was unrelievedly solemn and had no passion in him. He had at first rejected the role, saying he was weary of playing costume dramas, and he was sure that *Anna Karenina* would be a box-office failure because it was coming so close on the heels of a film based on Tolstoy's *Resurrection* with Anna Sten in the leading role. *Resurrection* had been a box-office failure; therefore, *Anna Karenina* would also be a failure. In addition, he was owned by Twentieth Century Pictures and there would be inevitable complications if he was loaned out. He entered the film without enthusiasm and continued to be unenthusiastic throughout its making.

Basil Rathbone, as Alexey Karenin, a high government official, was equally wooden and solemn. He sometimes appeared in a quilted dressing gown in the film, needing only a deerstalker hat to become Sherlock Holmes. One critic wrote that "he kept up a steady electric hum" like a refrigerator, but there was no electricity in him. If Fredric March was intolerable by reason of his total lack of interest in Garbo, which was odd behavior indeed since he had been cast as her lover, Basil Rathbone was intolerable because he was so prissily English in a role that demanded that the heavy-handed power of the Russian Empire should be observed in his least gestures. Basil Rathbone's chief fault was that he remained Basil Rathbone. Because Garbo's husband and lover were equally incompetent as supporting actors, the actress was left in a familiar predicament: In her own person she had to convey her distaste for a husband and her devotion to a lover. Because neither was worthy of her, she had somehow to suggest that she was deeply involved with them or with people like them, and she had to people our imagination with real

Anna Karenina, *with Fredric March*

presences rather than with fictions that seem to be made of cardboard. She succeeded superbly. Fredric March and Basil Rathbone vanished; in their places appeared presences summoned up by her imagination.

The philosopher Søren Kierkegaard was an avid theatre-goer, fascinated by the strange power of actors to suggest things that were quite simply invisible to the naked eye though visible to the eye of the imagination. At the Königstadter Theatre in Copenhagen he was especially attracted to a comic actor called Beckmann, who shuffled onto the stage in the tattered clothes of a tinker. He had come to a village and immediately began to engage the villagers in conversation. One saw the villagers emerging from their cottages: old men, women and children, lusty farm workers, young brides. He had a wink and a word for every one of them, roared with laughter, patted them on the back, did some tinkering work, addressed himself earnestly to the village mayor and to a flock of children, and they were all invisible. There was no village; no villagers had appeared; there was only the empty stage and the solitary actor in total command of the audience. It was not hypnotism. It was not a conjuring trick. Beckmann had summoned up an entire village by an act of the imagination.

So it was with Garbo in *Anna Karenina*. She summoned up presences that had no existence on the screen: a forthright, determined, and insanely jealous husband, a lover as flamelike as Romeo. Her beauty made them possible and inevitable. The camera, by exalting and magnifying her beauty, added to the illusion, but she was herself the illusionist. It was an art she practiced so unselfconsciously that she gave the impression of being artless. She was the sudden bowl of flowers that not only prolonged the emotion but created new emotions, wave after wave of emotions. She could have played the part of Anna Karenina without any supporting actors at all. Like Beckmann she could have stood on the empty stage and brought Vronsky and Karenin to life simply by an act of the imagination. Considering how incompetently she was served by Fredric March and Basil Rathbone, it might have been better if she had.

But it was not only the two male leads who were unenthusiastic. David Selznick, the producer of the film, was equally unenthusiastic. Disappointed with the box-office returns from *Queen Christina* and *The Painted Veil*, he decided at the last minute to abandon *Anna Karenina* and to replace it with a popular novel called *Dark Victory*, owned by his friend Jock Whitney. In a letter written to Garbo, who was staying at Palm Springs, he outlined the many reasons why *Anna Karenina* was doomed to failure while *Dark Victory* was certain to provide the long-hoped-for success. George Cukor was in agreement. Philip Barry was being approached to write the screenplay for *Dark Victory*. It would be

Anna Karenina, *with Freddie Bartholomew*

a simple matter to get started on the new project. Garbo's close friend Salka Viertel was asked to tell Garbo the story of *Dark Victory*, and Selznick hoped she would realize the advisability of abandoning a "heavy Russian drama" with "all the obvious pitfalls from the viewpoint of your millions of admirers." "I do hope," wrote Selznick, "you will not force us to proceed."

Garbo listened to the plea and rejected it. She did not like what she had heard about *Dark Victory*. She had immersed herself in *Anna Karenina* and it was now too late to make an abrupt turnabout. Her contract gave her the right to refuse to make a film if she disliked it, and there was nothing the studio could possibly do about it. After many delays *Anna Karenina* went before the cameras.

Clemence Dane, Salka Viertel, and S. N. Behrman were accomplished script writers, and in the normal course of events they might have produced a very good script. But they were under great pressure to produce a finished script in the shortest possible time, and none of them liked being rushed. The script is oddly unbalanced and betrays the fact that three people worked at it while another five or six people in the head office delivered judgment on it, re-sorted various incidents, and ordered additions wherever they felt that the film was not being sufficiently explicit or sufficiently devious in avoiding censure from the Hays Office, and they so affected the rhythm of the scenes that the film seems to move by fits and starts. Clarence Brown, whom Selznick regarded as a "masterly director," was entrusted with the direction, and this was a mistake. Selznick also insisted on the heavy pseudo-Russian atmosphere and vast panoramic scenes of feasting and dancing, and he was so taken with Freddie Bartholomew that he insisted on writing in extra scenes for him. Freddie Batholomew was not quite as wooden as Fredric March, but he possessed a fatuously prissy quality that was terribly jarring. It was beyond belief that he could have been Anna's son. Selznick was rather proud of the original writing of the scenes between Anna and her son, which had little enough basis in Tolstoy's novel. It was as though he had finally recognized that neither Basil Rathbone nor Fredric March could sustain a love passage with Garbo and that she was best served by the devotions of a child. Philippe de Lacy had played the role of Garbo's son to perfection in a brief scene in *Love*, and it was expected that little Freddie Batholomew would do as well. He did much worse, and succeeded in wrecking many scenes in the film.

Although the writing was incompetent and Clarence Brown's direction was uneven and sometimes grotesquely heavy-handed, Garbo was able to convey a credible Anna Karenina apparently without the slightest difficulty. She immersed herself so completely in the part that she

became Anna, and for once we are not so much blinded by her beauty as caught up in the silence of her tragedy. She is a creature of raging fires, and though we do not see the flames, we are aware of their shadows playing on her face. She can say quite obvious things and give them a weight of meaning they can scarcely bear. Her voice rises and falls with her emotions, while Karenin and Vronsky speak in flat, level tones, as if they were relating incidents in a football game that happened long ago. The sound track soars with Russian anthems, the screen is filled with officers in white uniforms, but the only person who looks Russian is Garbo.

The obvious faults of the film scarcely touch Garbo, for she is nearly faultless. She moves toward her doom with serene abandonment. "I see pain. I feel tears," she says in the film. "Why?" she is asked. "Because I am so happy." This is not what Anna says in the novel. Tolstoy saw her as much more mercurial, shifting from passion to hate and from affection to indifference, all in a moment. Garbo conveys these alterations with economy and superb finesse: her heavy eyelids are half lowered or she throws her lover a sidelong glance, and everything is said. Vronsky talks about his love for her, and it is all hollow in comparison with Anna's burning eyes. Only one thing is missing in Garbo's portrayal of Anna—her learning, a combination of scholarship and knowledge of practical matters. Vronsky on his estate acts as a paymaster, an engineer, an expert on forestry and the cultivation of crops. No one seeing Anna on the screen would think of her spending the day reading scientific books to help her lover. In the novel she is something of a bluestocking, a well-informed modern woman, capable of intelligent discussion on all subjects under the sun. She is practical and sensible, and therefore her infatuation with Vronsky is all the more unintelligible, even to Tolstoy, who saw her as a woman of quickly changing moods who remained fundamentally calm and sober. Indeed, her suicide in the novel is accomplished calmly and logically, as though she is solving a mathematical equation.

Garbo introduced into the film something wholly extraneous to the novel—a kind of passionate heroism. She looked heroic. She could portray an embattled saint, a warrior Queen, Artemis the Huntress, or Joan of Arc. She possessed the divine tenderness and flamelike abandon that melt all obstacles in their path. This was why the choice of Basil Rathbone and Fredric March proved to be so incongruous, for they refused to be melted, refused even to react to her. They were altogether too earthy for her, and her heroism was wasted on them.

Though the dialogue in the film version of *Anna Karenina* is flawed ("Love isn't everything. I am sick and tired of love," says Vronsky), it is not of very great importance. What Garbo says and what the other actors say is immaterial, for she carries the entire play on her shoulders. We see her walking wide-eyed to her doom, almost unaware of the presence of other people, alone in all the immensity of Russia, and she seems to represent, not Anna Karenina only, but all the transient beauty of the world. In retrospect the film seems to have fallen away from her, and we remember only the close-ups of her face, charged with such purity and radiance that we can recall every detail of it a quarter of a century later. She who had been so young in *Queen Christina* had now reached maturity. She seemed to have the power to change her age at will, to be protean in the forms of her beauty. In her next film she would be a courtesan who died young, scarcely out of her teens. Garbo would portray the fragility of her youth and the violence of her fever in the most miraculous of all her performances.

Anna Karenina remains a flawed film, appallingly directed, badly staged, with a cast of nearly incompetent performers. Nevertheless it is a masterpiece, for in spite of everything, Garbo succeeded in portraying a completely credible, beautiful, and desirable Anna Karenina.

Camille

Cover her face: mine eyes dazzle:
she died young.
    —JOHN WEBSTER,
        The Duchess of Malfi

WHEN ALEXANDRE DUMAS wrote the novel and then the play *Camille*, he was describing a woman he knew well, for she had been his mistress. She was one of the reigning beauties of Paris, renowned for her wit, her courage, the number of her lovers, and the enormous amount of money that passed through her hands. They said she had a strange power of entering a room quietly, and suddenly all the heads of the men would turn in her direction. They said, too, that there was something magical about her, that she bewitched people with a glance and that she was capable of rejuvenating the old. Her symbol was the white camellia, the flower and the leaves, which she wore at her breast.

Her real name was Alphonsine Plessis, and she was born in 1824 to Marin Plessis and Marie Deshayes. Marin was a scoundrel and a wastrel; Marie was descended through her mother from the minor aristocracy of Normandy. Marin abandoned his wife after giving her two daughters, and Alphonsine was brought up in great poverty. She was about fourteen when she came to Paris, where she worked in a dressmaker's establishment, and about sixteen when she became the mistress of a restaurant owner in the Palais Royal. Already her beauty was beginning to be

Marie Duplessis

talked about. It was not an ordinary beauty; there was something disquieting about it. She had enormous eyes, which were almond-shaped and unusually brilliant, a long classical nose, lips that curved up at the edges, and a pointed chin, which in any other woman would have seemed both too pointed and too powerful. Her skin was white and pink, and seemed translucent. She had a small waist, a swanlike neck, and she wore her hair in long ringlets that fell below her shoulders, framing her face. She looked more like a princess than a country girl from Normandy, and there was about her an extraordinary air of distinction, so that she gave the impression of having just stepped away from some magical place of her own to walk through the streets of Paris.

Soon Alphonsine Plessis changed her name. Because "Alphonsine" was a very bourgeois name and "Plessis" could belong to anyone, she became Marie Duplessis, which hinted at aristocratic origins. The restaurant owner was permitted to set her up in a small apartment in the Rue de l'Arcade near the Palais Royal, but not for long. The nineteen-year-old Antoine Agenor, Duc de Guiche, had just resigned from the army. Possessing a fortune and determined to be the reigning dandy and the greatest authority on all the beautiful women of his time, he carried Marie off, gave her an apartment, sat beside her in triumph in his box at the Opera, and set about giving her an education. She never learned to spell, but she learned to read and proudly displayed her library, which contained the works of Rabelais, Cervantes, Molière, Hugo, and Scott. She had evidently read them, for she talked about them at length, and very sensibly. She held a salon, which was attended by the Duc de Guiche's aristocratic friends and also by the most famous literary people of the time. She was admired, loved, and toasted. She spent money with prodigality. She had exquisite taste. She never engaged in backbiting, was always vivacious and high-spirited, and even her mounting debts did not dismay her. The Duc de Gramont, father of the young Duc de Guiche, disliked her and feared that she would ruin his son. Antoine Agenor was therefore sent on a grand tour of Italy, and Marie Duplessis became the mistress of the aging Comte de Stackelberg, a former Russian Ambassador, who gave her an apartment in the Boulevard de la Madeleine. As for Antoine Agenor, who eventually married a dour Scotswoman and settled down to a career in the foreign service of France under Napoleon III, it can be said with some certainty that if he had never lived, our present miseries would be lessened, for he was the French Foreign Minister who precipitated the Franco-Prussian War of 1870.

Marie Duplessis continued to live with the Comte de Stackelberg and to have as many lovers as she pleased. Among them was Alexandre Dumas, the son of the more famous Alexandre Dumas père. The young man was twenty years old, poor, elegant, talented, head over heels in love with her. They met secretly, though they sometimes abandoned secrecy altogether by occupying a box at the Théâtre des Variétés, parading their love affair publicly, and then going off to dinner in one of the well-publicized restaurants before returning to the apartment on the Boulevard de la Madeleine where the white vases were filled with camellias, where the leather-bound books gleamed in the candlelight, and where an enormous bed raised on feet shaped like gilded fauns and bacchantes gave promise of intoxicating nights. "She is one of those rare courtesans who has a heart," he wrote. But she was also very expensive, and there came a time when he could not afford her. "What is happening?" she wrote, when he failed to come to her. "Why do you send me no news of yourself? Why do you not write frankly? I hope you will write, and I hope to kiss you very tenderly, whether as a mistress or as a friend I leave to you to decide. Whatever your decision, I shall always be your devoted—Marie."

At midnight on August 30, 1845, Alexandre Dumas finally broke with her after a liaison that had lasted eleven months. "Let us both forget," he wrote. "Please forget a name that cannot mean much to you, and I will forget a happiness that is no longer possible for me. A thousand memories." But though he broke away, he felt continually attached to her.

Other lovers followed. Franz Liszt fell in love with her briefly and toyed with the idea of accompanying her on a journey to the Orient. The Comte de Perregaux took her to London and married her in a civil ceremony, which, it appears, had no legal standing in France. She was suffering from consumption. Her cheeks were flushed, there were fevers, she was spitting blood. She went off to watering places in Germany, drank five bottles of milk a day, and grew worse. She returned to her Paris apartment, sold her jewelry piece by piece, prayed frequently at an elaborate *prie-dieu* upholstered in velvet and ornamented with two gilt Virgins, and sometimes, wrapped in a red cashmere shawl, she leaned out of the window to watch the fashionable world walking and riding in the Boulevard de la Madeleine. She was pale and emaciated, her cheeks sunken, looking like the ghost of herself. It was winter, a cold rain was falling, her consumption grew worse, and she finally took to her bed. She died on February 3, 1847, at the height of the Carnival when all Paris danced in the streets. She had lived a full life, spent about half a million gold francs, and had a hundred lovers. She was twenty-two years old.

Marie Duplessis, known in her lifetime as *La Dame aux Camélias*, entered legend. Songs were sung about her; those who had known her wrote their reminiscences; her features were remembered in engravings showing her bare-shouldered, wearing a white gown, an ermine stole draped negligently over her arms, with a huge camellia at her breast. She wore a coronet, and there hovered over her lips a smile of the purest benediction. She was perhaps the most beautiful woman of her time.

Alexandre Dumas was in Algiers when she died, and it was some time before he learned of her death. He came to Paris, haunted the places where he had accompanied her, and wrote his novel *La Dame aux Camélias*, which was an immediate success. The novel was followed by a play, which was equally successful. He changed names, altered some situations, made her more deeply religious than she was, but preserved the special qualities that were truly hers. Her beauty, her vivacity, her gentleness, her goodness of heart, her delight in wild parties—all these are faithfully reflected in the novel. Because so many of her lovers were still alive, it was necessary to change her name to Marguerite Gautier, but he had not changed her character. It was an astonishing novel and an equally astonishing play, and because Dumas was writing about someone he had known and genuinely loved, there were freshness and tenderness in the writing that have power to move us. Marguerite Gautier, coughing out her life, white as a sheet and wholly beautiful, belongs among the great figures of fiction, and like all the great fictional characters she was modeled on a living person.

For Garbo *La Dame aux Camélias* was a superb vehicle. She too was a great beauty from a working-class background, famous and adored, possessing the "goodness of heart" that both Franz Liszt and Alexandre Dumas found in Marie Duplessis. There was even a physical resemblance between them, and Garbo's throaty voice admirably served to convey the huskiness of a consumptive's speech. She could, and did, step into the role without any difficulty. For a generation of filmgoers she became *La Dame aux Camélias*, and it was impossible to imagine anyone else playing the role.

Of course everything that could possibly go wrong went wrong. The script by Zoë Atkins was flat. The stage sets designed by Cedric Gibbons were grotesquely elaborate, heavy, and cluttered. Gibbons once announced that it was not necessary to seek literal accuracy in backgrounds; it was enough to suggest a period atmosphere with a few well-chosen props. But this time he surpassed himself with props: chandeliers, carved chairs, mahogany tables, four-poster beds, monumental doorways, tapestries. Marguerite Gautier's apartment might be taken for a room in a palace. With so much bric-a-brac on the set, there seemed to be a conspiracy to distract the spectators' attention from the presence of Garbo, who was outfitted by Gilbert Adrian in costumes so heavy that it was necessary to erect ice coolers on the set to prevent her from fainting. Garbo wore costumes that have very little in common with the costumes of the 1840s. They too were grotesquely elaborate and cluttered. It does not matter. She became Marguerite Gautier, sailed through all the rubbish on the set as though it did not exist, and dominated the picture.

She was lucky in her director, George Cukor, who directed with a light hand, permitted her to do very much as she pleased, and sometimes accepted her suggestions. There is a scene in the theatre where Marguerite Gautier walks through a lobby full of top-hatted dandies to display herself, for the courtesan continually has to sell herself. Cukor wanted her to walk slowly, so that the men's eyes would have time to linger on her. Instead she walked fast, in the knowledge that a beautiful woman has no need to walk slowly to attract men's attention. A prostitute walks slowly from one lamppost to another; a beautiful courtesan is more likely to walk quickly so that men will have only a fleeting glimpse of her. Garbo had thought out the implications of the scene; Cukor had not.

Because he was by far the most intelligent of Hollywood directors and was well aware of Garbo's abilities as an actress, Cukor interfered as little as possible in the film. With Garbo playing the leading role, it scarcely needed any direction. Irving Thalberg, the production chief at MGM, visited the set early in the shooting and observed that something quite new had happened. "Don't you understand, she is completely *unguarded*," he said. Now it seemed for the first time that the prickling defenses were down and she no longer felt it necessary to be on guard. She was enjoying herself; the part fitted her to perfection; she had never been more beautiful. A few days after visiting the set, Irving Thalberg died suddenly at the age of thirty-seven. His death, on September 14, 1936, filled the studio with gloom. Ironically, this gloom helped to set the appropriate mood for *Camille*.

Both Sarah Bernhardt and Eleonora Duse had played the role of Marguerite Gautier, and Garbo felt she was in good company. There survive to this day a few feet of film showing Bernhardt in the stage play. She waves her arms, stamps about on her one good leg, moves jerkily from one side of the stage to the other, and raises her eyes to heaven whenever fate deals her an unkind blow. No doubt the part was played with the same passionate intensity when it was first performed in 1854. Garbo deliberately underplayed her role with startling effect, for the more she underplayed it, the more intensity was generated. When fate deals unkind blows to her, she retreats quietly into herself, withdraws into a shuddering silence. When the father of Armand Duval begs her to give up his son, she agrees wordlessly and conveys her grief and horror over the separation by sinking to her knees very slowly and throwing her arms over a table. The scene is played like a slow dance, like a pavane, and is all the more successful because it is unexpected. George Cukor was surprised by the gesture. She had been asked only to register despair.

Robert Taylor in Camille

Instead she registered grief, the slow surrendering of her body to a despair so terrible that all her muscles were unstrung.

She was not helped by Lionel Barrymore, who played the role of Armand's father as though he were delivering speeches to Rotarians, nor by the setting, which was a cottage erected on a studio lot by people who had never been in a cottage and therefore had no idea what a cottage looked like. Garbo had to carry the whole weight of these scenes. Robert Taylor, grotesquely painted to resemble a male mannequin, pretty enough to decorate a chocolate box, was a pathetically insubstantial lover. Only Henry Daniell, as the icily contemptuous Baron de Varville, carried enough weight to be credible. He had the elegance of manner and the humanity to serve as a worthy foil. In the entire course of her film career, he was the only man who could effectively stand up to her.

Henry Daniell was an excellent actor who had the advantage of looking as though he had stepped out of the period of *La Dame aux Camélias*. His face, his manner, his way of walking, the ease with which he wore his elaborate costume, even his dreadful silences suggested the aristocrat. He could have played a Regency buck or King Louis XIV to perfection; he could have portrayed a credible Julius Caesar. He was a controlled and accomplished actor, and he slipped into the role of the Baron de Varville with what appeared to be the greatest of ease. In fact he was atrociously nervous throughout and terrified by the prospect of acting opposite Garbo. When George Cukor introduced a new scene, which showed the Baron returning unexpectedly at night to Marguerite Gautier's apartment while she is entertaining Armand Duval (who slips away only just in time), Henry Daniell was torn by many anxieties. It was a difficult scene to play. Worse still, the script called for Garbo to sit down at the piano and play for him, and then while she played, they would both break out in a kind of hard-edged hysterical laughter, for each had penetrated the other's secrets and found relief in laughter. Daniell met Garbo on the set and asked her what she thought of the new scene. She said it was difficult, and asked him what he thought.

"I think it is a good scene, but I am terribly worried about it," he replied. "You see, I don't laugh very easily."

"Neither do I," Garbo admitted.

Nevertheless the scene played well: The sudden bursts of fierce laughter came naturally, and there was a very rare sense of intimacy between them, for they played brilliantly to each other. The only other occasion when a real sense of intimacy was established was in the scene in *Queen Christina* when Garbo finds herself alone in a vast room with John Gilbert, munches grapes, and dallies with him in a rather offhand but

Henry Daniell and Greta Garbo

Robert Taylor and Greta Garbo

very pleasing manner. The electricity, so rarely generated, flowed out of the screen most memorably when she was with Henry Daniell.

In all her acting there was a certain element of detachment, an intellectual coolness. She was always the statue, very conscious of herself, a little remote from the world, aware that she was standing on a pedestal. Some of this came from her insecurity, the knowledge that she was a stranger in a foreign land, but it came too from her training in the Royal Dramatic Academy at Stockholm, where the pupils were taught to regard themselves as dedicated beings living apart from the world, beholden to nothing save their art. The tragic actress steps forth across the stage as though she has just descended from another world; she has little to do with the real world; she is half a goddess. This is why the scene in *Queen Christina* and the strange laughing scene in *Camille* have such a powerful effect. Suddenly "half a goddess" becomes a woman.

George Cukor, watching her closely on the set, arrived at some inevitable conclusions. He was fascinated by her regal bearing, her *plastique*, her intense and at the same time relaxed concentration. She never troubled to see the rushes, and this puzzled him, for he expected that she would attempt as a dedicated actress to learn from her mistakes. When he asked her why she refused to see them, she answered, "I have some idea, some notion of what I am doing, and every time I see it, it falls so short that it throws me." But this was only part of the explanation. She was living the part, thinking deeply about it, inventing her own ways of playing it, and the daily study of the rushes would have been distracting. It would have been an interruption of her concentrated study of her role. At all costs she was determined not to dissipate her energies. She did not stand around the set while the lights were being fixed and while the director and the scriptwriter went into conference. Instead, she wandered away to a little screened-off place where she could sunbathe and completely relax. She had excellent manners, told jokes, was friendly with the electricians, knew exactly what she wanted, laughed a good deal, and remained, as always, strangely remote, as though she were separated from the rest of the world by an invisible glass wall. "She was very funny and sweet, and I think fairly happy," Cukor concluded. Because she was living the role of Marguerite Gautier, the question of happiness scarcely arose. She saw herself as a woman doomed to die while still young. She sank into the role, lost herself in it, and was splendidly indifferent to anything else. She became Marguerite Gautier, and—what was even more important—she became Marie Duplessis, for she read everything she could find about that intoxicating person. She was in fact much closer to Marie Duplessis than to the character depicted by Dumas, who for mysterious reasons of his own made her repent her sins. Marie

Duplessis did repent, but only a little. She enjoyed life too much to see any advantage in repentance.

Cukor also observed, with mingled bewilderment and admiration, how Garbo instinctively achieved the most graceful solutions. There is a moment during the gambling scene when she drops her fan and the Baron de Varville orders her to pick it up. It is a moment of fierce, silent antagonism, yet it is necessary that it should be played quickly, almost fleetingly. Garbo did not bend down, did not surrender her dignity, did not break the flow of movement. She leaned sideways in a most beautiful way, as though performing a kind of dance, scooped up the fan, swayed momentarily, and continued as though nothing had happened. It was a small scene, but for Cukor it was the purest magic.

Jules Janin, an eminent French literary and dramatic critic, who later became a member of the Académie Française, remembered the first time he met Marie Duplessis. He was sitting with Franz Liszt in the green room of one of the theatres on the Boulevards. The green room was badly lit, crowded, and boisterous. There were critics, writers, dramatists, musicians, theatrical and professional people, all passing the time away before the prompter's three knocks announced that the curtain was about to go up. Suddenly, to the intense surprise of everyone in the room, there entered an apparition more radiant than a Queen. It was winter, the floor was muddy, a log fire was burning. The apparition stepped across the mud and advanced straight to the table where Liszt and Janin were sitting close to the fireplace. She sat down next to Liszt and murmured that she had once heard him play and it had set her dreaming. The three knocks were heard. Everyone except Liszt, Janin, and the stranger went off to take their seats in the theatre. Liszt, amazed by the regal presence of the young woman, wondered whether he had been presented to her at a levee in London or in the town house of the Duchess of Sutherland. Janin, writing many years afterward, remembered every detail of her costume: her gloves, her handkerchief trimmed with costly lace, her silk stockings, her petticoats, and he remembered too that she wore enormous pearl earrings worthy of an Empress. But who was she? She gave no hint. A countess? A princess? She spoke with an exquisite delicacy and with just a suggestion of hauteur as befitted a lady of the court. Liszt was entranced and Janin was intrigued. They went on talking all through the third act of the play, very happy together, and then she vanished.

Janin saw her again about a year later at the Opera. By this time she was famous, and he knew her name. Her beautiful black, ringletted hair was festooned with diamonds and flowers; her arms and bosom were bare; she wore a white dress, a crimson cloak, and a necklace of emeralds. The cloak was lined with ermine, and the dress had evidently cost a fortune. She seemed to be suffering from lassitude, bored by her current lover, indifferent to her admirers. Janin found himself wondering whether she was enjoying the role she played. He remembered the words of Ninon de l'Enclos, a friend of the Prince de Condé and Madame de Maintenon, who said, "Had anyone proposed formerly to me to lead such a life as I have led, I should have died of grief and terror!"

Janin saw her for the third and last time in Brussels at the gala opening of the Paris-Brussels railroad. The huge railroad station was filled to capacity with French, Belgian, Dutch, Spanish, and German dignitaries. Kings and queens were in attendance; everybody who was anybody was present in the station, which for the occasion was transformed into a kind of garden filled with trees, flowers, flags, and banners. Nothing more colorful had ever been assembled. Suddenly Marie Duplessis appeared, pale, radiant, already dying. It appeared that no one had invited her. Her entrance card was her imperial beauty. Soon she abandoned her escort, found someone who pleased her among a crowd of dancers, and began to waltz. "She danced marvelously, neither too quickly nor stooping too much, obeying the guidance she felt inwardly, keeping perfect time and scarcely touching the earth with her light feet."

This is precisely the quality that Garbo gave to the film: No one had ever acted so imperially on the screen. In *Camille*, which is her masterpiece, she dominated by her sheer presence, by the splendor of her being, so that it became impossible to believe that she was Marguerite Gautier, a courtesan dying of consumption; there was Garbo playing the game of being a courtesan, playing it so well that we sometimes believed that she believed she was acting a role, but we who knew better were aware that at last the quintessential Garbo had been revealed. Aficionados who studied her films minutely compared certain gestures in *Camille* with similar gestures in *Gösta Berlings Saga*, and they remembered that she was more queenly in *Camille* than she had ever been in *Queen Christina*. She had at last reached the heights, and they wondered if she could ever perform so well again.

Some of the credit must go to George Cukor because he respected her as an actress and let her go her own way, and to Gilbert Adrian, not for his design of her clothes but for insisting that Garbo should wear real diamonds and emeralds because perfect beauty demanded perfect jewelry. He insisted, too, that at the beginning of the film she should be curled and ringletted and that gradually, as her life moved toward its end, there should be fewer curls and ringlets until at the end her hair

Robert Taylor and Greta Garbo

should be drawn back with classic severity. He gave her voluminous black cloaks (as though she were playing a melodrama), spangled her white chiffon dresses with silver stars (as though she were a ballet dancer), and placed fantastically large black velvet bows at her waist, which hinted too emphatically that she was doomed. He announced that he would dress her in white at the beginning, then she would pass through various shades of gray, and at the end she would wear the black of mourning. Happily, he did not keep to this silly pattern. He continually overdressed her, thus attracting the spectator's eye away from her, hoping perhaps that people would marvel at his dressmaking. But no one in his senses looks at Garbo's dresses.

Camille has the magic of perfection because Garbo acts perfectly at every moment. But there were disasters aplenty. Lionel Barrymore, as the father of Armand Duval, was made of pieces of wood that clacked and clattered; Robert Taylor gleamed like a wax dummy in a store window; Jessie Ralph, playing Nanine, the nurse, was a fusspot. But Prudence was marvelously played by Laura Hope Crews, and Henry Daniell played an impossibly difficult role with ease and intelligence. The disasters were outweighed by the achievements, and the crowning achievement was the death scene. Originally there were two death scenes, one with a long farewell speech, the other played in silence. Both were filmed. Mercifully the farewell speech was jettisoned; Marguerite Gautier dies almost in silence. She coughs, gives a strange little shudder, and it is all over. But in that cough and that shudder there was great art, great feeling, and great dignity.

While *Camille* was believable throughout, *Conquest* was never believable at all. Something went wrong very early in the production. Partly it was the unmanageable script to which at least five and perhaps twenty people contributed. We know the names of five people who had something to do with the script, for they are recorded in the screen credits: "Screen play by Samuel Hoffenstein, Salka Viertel, and S. N. Behrman from the novel *Pani Walewska* by Waclaw Gasiorowski and a dramatization by Helen Jerome." There were too many cooks in the kitchen, too many false starts and inexplicable changes of direction. Charles Boyer was not a very credible Napoleon, nor was it possible to believe that Marie Walewska was his mistress; nor was it possible to believe that the film had any real relation to the historical Napoleon.

Perhaps it was the heavy-handedness of Clarence Brown, who seemed to be out of sympathy with the Napoleonic era. Perhaps it was the absence of William Daniels, the cameraman who photographed nearly all of Garbo's films. Or else it was the appalling ineptitude of the casting director, who cast Dame May Whitty as the formidable mother of

Rex O'Malley and Greta Garbo

Napoleon and Scotty Beckett as Napoleon's son by Countess Walewska, thus reducing the scenes in which they appear to travesties. In *Camille* there was some disastrous casting, but so great was Garbo's radiance that no one was disturbed by it. In *Conquest* one noticed it all the time.

In theory the film should have been as successful as *Camille* and *Queen Christina*. These films dealt with historical personages who were sympathetic, adventurous, imaginative, caught up in hopeless love affairs. The real Marie Walewska was all these things. She was beautiful beyond reason, and Napoleon adored her; she had a son by him, was spurned by him, visited him on Elba, and lived all the remaining years of her life under his shadow. She, too, was sympathetic, adventurous, and imaginative, taking part in countless intrigues and always for the noble cause of preserving the freedom of Poland. In the film she is given no opportunity to show her mettle. Napoleon bellows at her like an aroused bull, upbraids her for not loving him enough, talks endlessly about his duties, and has not an atom of imperial grandeur. Fingers move along maps of Central Europe; dissolve to the battlefields; dissolve to cannon and smoke; dissolve to the impatient, bull-like Napoleon in his tent pacing restlessly, waiting for reports on his victories. He gestures too much and too often. In fact, the real Napoleon gestured very little and rebuked the actor Talma for his gestures in one of Corneille's plays, saying that a real Emperor knows that with a slight crook of a finger he can order men to be executed or to be thrown into battle. As Napoleon, Boyer was a disaster; he became just one more of those shadowy, unreal, and improbable lovers who dogged Garbo's film career. The script writers were incapable of fantasy. They clung to history, dates, battles, receptions in the palaces, orgies, soldiers. To her only brother, Paul, Marie says, "I love the Emperor. That's why I am here. You understand that, don't you?" Napoleon's mother tells her, "My son is not only an Emperor, he is also a man." Ordered by the Polish nobility to give herself to Napoleon for the sake of Poland, she says, "Are you suggesting that I can succeed where the Polish legions have failed?" It was very nearly the worst written of her scripts, and it came immediately after the best written. There was only one moment when the script came to life, and that was in a small scene played between the old Countess Pelagia and Napoleon. The Countess was played by Maria Ouspenskaya, formerly of the Moscow Art Theatre, a formidable actress and an extraordinary presence, for she was very tiny and nevertheless she towered over every actor who came near her. She has lost her memory and has no idea who Napoleon is. "Who are you, young man?" she asks. "I am Napoleon." "Napoleon who?" "Bonaparte." She insists that he play cards with her, and because he claims to be an Emperor, at least he can afford to play for

Conquest, *with Charles Boyer*

money. Inevitably he cheats. Inevitably she discovers him cheating. She throws down her cards and says, "You are nothing more than a cheating corporal."

But if *Conquest* has very little to commend it as a film, it has one supreme merit. There are many close-ups of Garbo. She appears to be lost in a dream in the midst of a senseless drama, as she wanders through the Napoleonic wars. The spectator lives from one close-up to another. The fiction that she is Marie Walewska is scarcely credible; it is easier to believe that she is still *La Dame aux Camélias*, who has strayed most inopportunely into the arms of a bigger and fatter Baron de Varville. *La Dame aux Camélias* is riding through a snowstorm on a sleigh, wearing wonderfully rich furs. (Garbo is always most beautiful when seen against the snow and the northern forests.) Suddenly Napoleon enters, absurdly jowly, complaining for the hundredth time about the burdens of high office, and though he stands in the center of the screen, he seems to be very small and his voice seems to come from far away.

Camille shows the heights Garbo could reach as an actress, but *Conquest* demonstrates only what we knew already—that Garbo was audaciously beautiful and was growing more beautiful every year. Her beauty was so dramatic that it is perfectly possible to imagine her alone on the screen, and it would have been a better film if she had simply narrated without the aid of maps or battle scenes what had happened to her in France and Poland. She could have whispered, "Napoleon," and he would have been all the more real because she had summoned him. She could have spoken of her child, and the child would have appeared in our imaginations as a real child, and we would not have been bothered with the pretty, curly-haired monstrosity presented to us. She needed few of the trappings provided by Hollywood. Least of all did she need those vast marble palaces, interminable ball scenes, and parades. She needed only the freedom to be beautiful, to tell stories, to demonstrate her powers as an actress. She did not need the extravaganzas.

With the shoddy material she was given, Garbo played with all her accustomed brilliance, and sometimes she even succeeded in convincing us that she was really Marie Walewska and that Napoleon was really Napoleon, but never for long. One remembers the film for those close-ups, which were always startling, even though they were familiar, and for the look of pity on her face when she contemplates Napoleon at the last. There was no diminution of her powers; she was trapped by a poverty-stricken script. The promise remained—the promise of roles greater than Camille and Anna Karenina, an entire galaxy of brilliant roles. She did not know and could not guess that she was very close to the end of her career as an actress.

Ninotchka

Comrades! People of the world!
The revolution is on the march . . .
but not yet, please—wait, wait—let
us be happy . . .
—From *Ninotchka*

WHEN NINOTCHKA was being filmed in the latter months of 1939,
no one could possibly have believed that Garbo's career would soon be
coming to an abrupt halt. She was at the height of her fame. She was
adored and cherished by millions, and over most of the world her name
was a household word. She was thirty-four, and seemed likely to enjoy
another twenty years of filmmaking. There are scenes in *Ninotchka*
where she looks eighteen, and there is never a moment when she looks
older than twenty-five. She was in good health, reasonably happy, disturbed only by the distant crises in Europe and the fear that Germany
would invade Sweden. More and more she was acting in films that gave
full play to her great talents. She was on the crest of the wave.

For the first time, with *Ninotchka*, she was presented with a script
that was worthy of her. She would never again be asked to say the imbe-
cile things she says in *Conquest*, or so it seemed. This was a film where
there were no shipwrecks, no ambiguities, no sustained passages of vulgarity. She was not required to act against the grain, and she was free at
last from being a vamp, a *femme fatale*, a stereotype. She could act all
the more honestly because she was free of her chains.

Felix Blessart, Greta Garbo, Sig Rumann, and Alexander Cranach

Ninotchka, her swan song, belonged to a brilliant new order of things. It was a satire, wildly funny, totally improbable. What it satirized was Garbo herself, or rather her legend: the cold northerner immune to marriage, solemn and self-absorbed. The film was gay, polished, and civilized, and had no message except that love-making and good food are the essential ingredients of life, a message that was already sufficiently well known. It laughed at the Czardom, the Soviet Union, and the democracies. In one especially absurd and beautiful passage, Garbo is seen laughing herself silly, one roar of laughter following on another—and the film was advertised with the words "GARBO LAUGHS!!!" as though this were a new and hitherto unknown aspect of her character now revealed to the public for the first time. The film opened on November 3, 1939. World War II was two months old, and the world was finding very few reasons for laughing.

Nevertheless the film came out at the right time and for all the right reasons. Its gaiety was heart-warming; its unpretentiousness was a relief. The film was calculated to banish all fears and nagging thoughts for a period of 110 minutes, and admirably succeeded in doing what it set out to do. The world of *Ninotchka* had very little to do with reality and was not the worse for that. Ernst Lubitsch, the director, was a master of spinning out comedy until it was as light and airy as spun candy. It is precisely that lightness and airiness that made the film so delectable.

The script was a composite effort by Charles Brackett, Billy Wilder, and Walter Reisch, and like nearly all composite efforts it should have ended in failure. In fact it succeeded in giving the impression of having been written by one man in a single weekend while surrounded by magnums of champagne.

The names of the characters are very odd inventions indeed. Garbo plays Ninotchka Yakushova, and while Ninotchka is an acceptable diminutive for Nina, Yakushova is not a Russian name and if it is derived from anything, it can only come from the Russian word *yak* meaning yak. The Grand Duchess Swana is another impossible invention, since the name Swana does not exist in Russian. Ninotchka's lover, played by Melvyn Douglas, is Count Léon d'Algout, who appears to be a descendant of the more famous Countess Marie d'Agoult, the beloved of Franz Liszt, although there is no explanation for the rearrangement of her aristocratic name. Iranoff, Bulianoff, and Kopalsky, the three stooges sent by the Soviet Government to find the Grand Duchess's jewels, have names that sound Russian but are not. We are warned from the beginning that this is a fantasy about a nonexistent country called the Soviet Union. This does not matter very much, because most of the action takes place in a nonexistent Paris. That the Paris of the film has no existence is made clear by the opening shot of the Place de la Concorde with the superimposed title: "THIS PICTURE TAKES PLACE IN PARIS IN THOSE WONDERFUL DAYS WHEN A SIREN WAS A BRUNETTE AND NOT AN ALARM . . . AND IF A FRENCHMAN TURNED OUT THE LIGHT IT WAS NOT ON ACCOUNT OF AN AIR RAID!" The exclamation point was provided by MGM.

This superimposed title is the only sad thing about the film, which begins quite properly with Iranoff, Bulianoff, and Kopalsky projecting themselves through revolving doors into the ultra-elegant Hotel Clarence. They set the tone and the pace of the film. They are three comics bent on mischief and conspiracy, and though they describe themselves as members of the Russian Board of Trade, we are under no illusion about their real origin in the slapstick comedies of the Mack Sennett era. They are a thoroughly disruptive influence and will, if given the least opportunity, tear down the Hotel Clarence and everything in it. They proceed to occupy the royal suite, the only suite left in the hotel worthy of such distinguished visitors. Bulianoff wonders whether Lenin would approve of them occupying this formidable suite, but Kopalsky provides the proper answer: "Are you the Bulianoff who fought on the barricades? And now you are afraid to take a room with a bath? If Lenin were alive, he would say, 'Bulianoff, Comrade, for once in your life you are in Paris!'" Bulianoff is beaten to the ground. "Who am I to contradict Lenin?" he replies, and on that happy note surrenders to the common cause.

The three clowns derive from the Mack Sennett comedies, but with a difference. Melchior Lengyel, who wrote the original story, Billy Wilder, who wrote most of the script, and Ernst Lubitsch, who directed the film, were all Central Europeans with a peculiarly Central European sense of humor. Billy Wilder was an Austrian, who had written screenplays in Berlin and worked as a director in Paris before coming to Hollywood. His three clowns therefore were far more explosive than the Keystone Cops, for they believed in their lunacies. Their madness exploded inwardly; they were genuinely happy only when they were dancing on the edge of a precipice. Ultimately they will bring everyone, including Garbo, into the magic circle of their insanity.

The Grand Duchess Swana, played by Ina Claire, is described as a Romanoff but lacks the Romanoff sense of dignity. Her origins, like her name, may be spurious; she is not entirely convincing; her love affair with Count Léon d'Algout is lukewarm; both of them have strayed from a Noel Coward comedy. They provide the pizzicato effects, the spluttering of the fuse, before the gunpowder blows up. They are very polished, and the three stooges exist in a world where polish is totally unnecessary for survival.

Enter Garbo, special envoy of the Soviet Government, empowered to bring order into the lives of the three stooges and to bring Communist good sense to bear on the various problems presented by the Grand Duchess's jewels, which are confiscated by the Soviets. Because she is Garbo, she arrives by train, emerging mysteriously amid gusts of steam onto the crowded platform, mysterious and remote, and she is in fact so mysterious and remote that Iranoff, Bulianoff and Kopalsky at first fail to recognize her as the plenipotentiary of the Soviet Government. One can hardly blame them, for in her severe clothes she resembles a stern schoolmistress. When a porter approaches to take her luggage, she is so ignorant of the ways of the Western world that she asks him why he is offering to help. "It is my business," the porter answers. "That is no business," she rebukes him. "That is social injustice." And when Bulianoff, somewhat disturbed by her domineering manner, asks how things are in Moscow, she replies, "Very good. The last mass trials were a great success. There are going to be fewer and better Russians."

Garbo, as schoolmistress and plenipotentiary, is wonderfully convincing. She even walks like a schoolmistress turned plenipotentiary. She goes directly to the heart of a problem, makes the appropriate logical deductions, and comes relentlessly to the inevitable Marxist conclusion. Seeing an absurd shape in a hotel showcase, she asks what it is. Told that it is a woman's hat, she replies, "How can such a civilization survive which permits women to put things like that on their heads? It won't be long now, Comrades!" And when by the purest chance she meets Count Léon d'Algout near the Place de la Concorde and very sensibly asks him the direction to the Eiffel Tower only to be met with a barrage of flirtatious remarks, she sniffs, "I have heard of the arrogant male in capitalist society. It is having a superior earning power that makes you like that. Your type will soon be extinct!"

Lubitsch enjoyed quick cutting, sudden changes of pace, short rushes of sophisticated dialogue. He intensely disliked explanatory dialogue and complex emotions. In *Ninotchka* not a single complex emotion is permitted to arise, every character belongs to a well-established type, and the film is as neatly packaged as a beribboned hatbox. That the decoration is absurd and wasteful, that the hatbox is more expensive than the hat, and that the backgrounds are the purest kitsch are not matters of any particular importance, for Lubitsch has accomplished his purpose, which is to give Garbo a freedom she never previously possessed. We watch with fascination while she tumbles head over heels in love with Melvyn Douglas. We do not believe she could possibly fall in love with Douglas, but that too is totally unimportant. The charade is played with civilized good humor, and neither Garbo nor Douglas is under any illusions about

the nature of the charade. The schoolmistress plenipotentiary becomes a woman in love, glowing with happiness, absurdly gay and unpredictable, and if we cannot quite believe that Douglas is her predestined lover, that too is to be expected—we never believed in any of her past lovers. Once again the film is Garbo, and all the rest is decoration.

But this time, and perhaps for the first time, the decoration is worthy of its subject. The luxurious hotel rooms provide the perfect background for a charade. A mythical Paris floats past. Occasionally we are permitted to hear authentic French accents. We see French taxicabs, the Eiffel Tower is outlined in lights, and we are reminded at all times that we are not in Hollywood but in some mythical kingdom called France. But this only adds to the necessary air of confusion, and is no more convincing than the banner on the Elizabethan stage that announces, "Here is Agincourt."

In the past the settings of Garbo's films were totally unbelievable. The cabin in *Susan Lenox*, the palace in *Queen Christina*, the grand staircase in *Anna Karenina*, the cabin in *Anna Christie*—all had the appearance of having been slapped together inexpertly by studio carpenters. During the scenes when Garbo was not present, the eye would find itself straying over those painted walls and there would come the sensation that they were about to fall with a resounding crash, and perhaps it would be better if they did fall. But in *Ninotchka*, as in *Grand Hotel*, there was a curious sense of substantiality. We do not require a luxury hotel that it should have substance; it is as gaudy and as irrelevant as the icing on a wedding cake. And simply because we do not demand substance, we take it for what it is, and are satisfied with it, and accept it with absolute conviction. The Hotel Clarence, an imaginary hotel in an imaginary city, achieves a kind of monumentality.

Lubitsch was at ease in luxury hotels, for he had spent a good part of his life in them. He loved them and detested them, was bored by them and enchanted by them. He knew exactly how they operated and had no more respect for them than a plumber has for bathroom pipes. Because he was so much at ease in these hotels, he had no difficulty maneuvering his characters through its endless corridors, and because he tended to see life from the point of view of the hotel servants, we are sometimes given a servant's-eye view of the characters. Thus when Iranoff, Bulianoff, and Kopalsky throw a luncheon party to celebrate their successes, we never see them. Instead we see two waiters pushing a cart piled high with a gargantuan display of food; they pause outside the suite; they knock; the door opens; we hear a tremendous chorus of approval. A moment later a cigarette girl comes swaying along the corridor, and there is another knock, and another loud chorus of approval. The waiters back away

Greta Garbo and Melvyn Douglas

from the suite with an empty cart, the cigarette girl comes hurrying out, a little flushed with surprise and excitement, and this is followed by a quick dissolve. When we see the cigarette girl again, she is accompanied by two other girls. All three vanish into the suite, and this time the chorus of approval reaches tumultuous proportions. Iranoff, Bulianoff, and Kopalsky are all the more present because they are invisible.

Lubitsch was a master of sleight-of-hand. He would demonstrate convincingly that he had nothing up his sleeve, and a moment later he would pull out three pigeons, two hundreds yards of colored ribbons, sixteen flags, and four balloons. He could do such things so quietly, so disarmingly that it was impossible to take offense. It was even more breathtaking when he pulled Garbo and Douglas out of his sleeve.

The conjurer knows that he must act quickly and maintain an endless flow of distracting patter. So it was in *Ninotchka*. The spectator finds himself puzzled by a phenomenon never observed in previous Garbo films—the action moves forward at the speed of an express train. *Camille* and *Anna Karenina* moved at the leisurely pace of hansom cabs, and even *Queen Christina* sometimes descends to a walking pace. In *Ninotchka* for the first time we are aware that everything is hurrying toward a conclusion, even though the conclusion is certain to be unsatisfactory and chaotic. In fact the conclusion takes place in a wholly unbelievable Constantinople, where Ivanoff, Bulianoff, and Kopalsky have opened a restaurant for the purpose of serving their country and making friends, and also so that they can bring about a rendezvous between Ninotchka and Count Léon d'Algout. The restaurant is the sheerest subterfuge. We are back again among painted slats, this time combined with back projections of Constantinople. It does not matter. The film has moved so rapidly and with so much assurance up to this point that we no longer care what happens as long as Ninotchka and her Count are reconciled at last. If the film had ended on an iceberg floating in the South Pacific, we would not care and we would be equally happy.

Ninotchka had speed, elegance, forthrightness, lunatic comedy. As a commentary on the Soviet Union, which had just witnessed a bloodbath of unprecedented proportions, it made no sense whatsoever. It offered no solutions, raised no problems, asked no questions. Yet it touched one of the most unfathomable of life's mysteries—the childlike gaiety that lies somewhere at the heart of the universe. From time to time, amid the solemn dissonances of Beethoven's posthumous quartets, we hear snatches of childlike song. So in *Ninotchka*, despite all the tinsel trappings, the overstuffed boudoirs, the glittering mirrors, the thick pile carpets, and the relentless artificiality of the plot, the spirit of pure comedy sometimes erupts and seems to burst into snatches of song. The comedy

is not so much verbal as lyrical. It is to be found in the way this assemblage of clowns dances and leaps across the stage.

Yet the lunatic words were often beguiling and wonderfully matched in their absurdity the absurd characters. Here, for example, the Count is explaining that he is an old-fashioned bourgeois and cannot therefore accept Ninotchka's theory that love is a purely chemical phenomenon:

NINOTCHKA: I used to belong to the petty bourgeoisie myself. My mother and father wanted me to stay and work on the farm, but I preferred the bayonet.

LÉON *(baffled and surprised):* The bayonet? Did you really?

NINOTCHKA: I was wounded before Warsaw.

LÉON: Wounded? How?

NINOTCHKA: I was a sergeant in the Third Cavalry Brigade. Would you like to see my wound?

LÉON: I'd love to.

NINOTCHKA *(pulling up sleeve and showing wound)*: A Polish lancer. I was sixteen.

LÉON: Poor Ninotchka. Poor, poor Ninotchka.

NINOTCHKA: Don't pity me. Pity the Polish lancer. After all, I'm still alive.

So she was—quiveringly alive! The line, spoken with such conviction and yet thrown away so carelessly, demonstrated her mastery of comedy. She relished the role and played it to the hilt. It was a new experience, and wonderfully invigorating. Not all the best comic lines were given to her; they were shared equally among all the actors. Here is the Count expatiating on the pleasures of love:

LÉON: Why do snails, the coldest of creatures, circle interminably around each other? Why do moths fly hundreds of miles to find their mates? Why do flowers slowly open their petals? Oh, Ninotchka, Ninotchka, surely you feel some slight symptom of the divine passion? A general warmth in the palms of your hands? A strange heaviness in your limbs? A burning of the lips that isn't thirst but a thousand times more tantalizing, more exalting, than thirst?

NINOTCHKA: You are very talkative.

LÉON *(kissing her)*: Was that talkative?

NINOTCHKA: No, that was restful. Again.

Comedy has a mischievous way of spinning on a word, and the word "Again" was at once comic, improbable, and wildly appropriate. The love affair continues its madcap course through the curious adventure of

the Grand Duchess Swana's jewels. Ninotchka goes to a working-class restaurant and in her puritanical fashion orders a serving of raw carrots and beets. The Count follows her, sits beside her, professes to be a habitué of the restaurant, hails the workingmen around him and is properly gratified when they respond to him. He tries to make her smile, telling one hopeless joke after another, and fails to produce the least crack in her armor. Finally he gives up in despair and while moving to another table, trips and falls. Then at last Ninotchka bursts out in peals of laughter.

It is one of the more famous moments in the film, but the discerning spectator will note that the peals of laughter are not synchronized with her lip movements. In fact, Garbo rocked with laughter and made all the appropriate movements but was completely unable to laugh aloud. Her laughter was manufactured for her by the sound department. Though she could not bring herself to laugh aloud, she smiled winningly and enjoyed herself, taking pleasure in the lines that had been artfully created for her.

One day the Count offers to crown her Grand Duchess of the People with Swana's tiara. She asks, "Is it the wishes of the masses?" Told that the masses will be satisfied with nothing less, Ninotchka says, "Thank you, Léon. Thank you, masses." She accepts the crown and then turns to the assembled invisible masses to deliver her acceptance speech through fumes of champagne: "Comrades! People of the world! The revolution is on the march, the wars will wash over us, bombs will fall, all civilization will crumble—but not yet, please—wait, wait—let us be happy—give us our moment!" The speech delivered by Ninotchka Yakushova, "a tiny cog in the great wheel of revolution," was at least more sensible than many speeches delivered by real dictators. She was carried to bed, still wearing her tiara, with a happy smile playing on her lips. "So happy and so tired," she murmurs with her arms around the Count's neck. This is no longer social comedy. Here was the abandonment of one role for another role, the transformation of the commissar was complete, and Melvyn Douglas carrying Garbo in his arms might be the most enviable of men, but he was also the only actor who ever carried her in his arms convincingly. The scene was contrived, but in its contrivance there was great tenderness.

It was Lubitsch's custom every morning to assemble the actors and discuss their roles with them. Because he was both producer and director he was in a position of quite extraordinary authority. He chose, for good reason, not to exert his authority. Garbo, Douglas, and Ina Claire were unusually intelligent actors; they knew at every moment what they were doing; they did not need to be instructed in their art. Their roles, which

seemed to flow so effortlessly, were in fact extremely difficult. Douglas was given an almost impossible task; he paced each scene, took command of Garbo, and at the same time had to give the impression of submitting to her, of being her foil, feeding her with those questions that received the appropriate noncommittal replies. In this way throughout the film he was the warming fire that coaxed her into life. "Do you like me just a little bit?" he asks her, and she replies, "You are not entirely distasteful to me." Garbo, too, has a difficult task, for her words have to be said both lightly and soberly, with just the faintest trace of resignation and amusement. Everything would have been lost if she had been too emphatic, if she seemed to be delivering the line for a laugh. Ina Claire, humor crackling from her fingertips, more Grand than Duchess, her quick mind alert for all the shades of humorous interpretation, agrees to relinquish her claim to the jewels if the Count is given back to her. This, too, was difficult to act, but she succeeded admirably. Lubitsch's task was perhaps the easiest. Given the kind of script he wanted, he had only to guide his actors gently to get the best out of them.

Ninotchka was a triumph of high spirits and decency. It even had a message, which was precisely the message declaimed by Garbo when she was tipsy. It had two minor blemishes—an absurd scene in which Ninotchka addresses a small bedside photograph of Lenin, saying, "Smile, little father," whereupon the stern Lenin is seen beaming with pleasure, and the rather hurried and inelegant ending, with Constantinople achieving a monumental incoherence. Constantinople deserved better. So did the actors who, up to that point, had performed with elegance and distinction. In his haste to bring Ninotchka and the Count together at the end, Lubitsch defied the accumulated logic of his story. In this he emulated the authors of the Restoration comedies, which he had studied exhaustively. In Restoration comedies all relationships become so tangled that in the last five minutes a hopelessly unacceptable resolution is imposed on the plot. So it was with *Ninotchka*. At the end there was an inconsequential dance, a kicking up of heels, complete abandonment.

MGM was so pleased with the success of *Ninotchka* that it was decided to put Garbo and Douglas into another social comedy. It was called *Two-faced Woman* and was based on a play by Ludwig Fulda. George Cukor, who had made *Camille*, was chosen as the director. He disliked the title, the script, the plot, and the theme, but felt that he had to obey orders. MGM had decided that henceforth Garbo could play comedy roles, and what could be more comic than Garbo playing twin sisters? Advertisements proclaimed her the "lively lady" in *Ninotchka*; now she would be doubly lively. Halfway through the film, Cukor real-

Two-faced Woman, *with Melvyn Douglas*

ized that he was confronted with a total disaster—a film so ragged, repetitive, and incoherent that it would have been better if everyone had simply stopped work and gone home.

Two-faced Woman was not an ordinary disaster: It was a monumental debacle. Everything went wrong from the beginning. The atmosphere in the studio was funereal. The actors went on performing because they were troupers, because there was just a faint possibility that the general stupidity of the film would be redeemed by the lightness of the comedy, and above all because the machine had been set in motion and could not be stopped. During the making of *Camille* and even more during the making of *Ninotchka*, there had been a feeling of euphoria on the set, for everyone knew he was creating a film that was imaginative and intelligent and therefore worthwhile, whatever happened at the box office. *Two-faced Woman*, being neither imaginative nor intelligent, was certainly not worth doing, and everyone knew it.

The fault lay largely with the studio's publicity people. Someone, having read the lighthearted script, convinced himself that the film had come about in order to introduce a new Garbo to the world—Garbo the pure comedian, mistress of the offhand wisecrack, the new woman, witty and sensual, no longer aloof. She had an athletic body, and therefore she would be represented as an athlete when she played the role of Karin Blake and as a svelte, luxury-loving woman of the world when she played Karin's twin sister. As an athlete she would be seen swimming vigorously and speeding effortlessly down ski slopes. As a woman of the world she would be shown attracting men as flypaper attracts flies, pitting one against another, vamping them to death. The publicity people were enjoying themselves. No one else was enjoying himself.

George Cukor, who first came to Hollywood as a speech director to advise actors long accustomed to silent films about how to speak, was normally loquacious and delighted in discussing actors' roles. But it was observed that he kept his discussions to the minimum and his direction was perfunctory. Normally, if actors intensely disliked the way a scene was written in the script, he would alter it according to their wishes or so modify it that there would be nothing to offend them. He trusted his actors, knew them well, and recognized that they knew a great deal about acting. Garbo intensely objected to a scene where she is seen swimming in the hotel pool and coming out of the water. She had good reasons for objecting. The scene is pointless, having nothing whatsoever to do with the story; it was devised by the script writers to show her in near nudity. With her lean, muscular body, she was not a bathing beauty, and she felt strongly that the scene was totally unnecessary. She asked Cukor to leave it out. He said, "It has to go in." She accepted his

order reluctantly but was unable to suppress a look of hurt and anger. She began to feel that MGM, for some unknown reason, had embarked on a conspiracy to destroy her. She was more than hurt, more than angry. Everything about the film suggested that she was being wasted.

Cukor's peremptory manner and Melvyn Douglas's obvious distaste for some of the scenes disturbed her. About half the film consists of dialogue between Garbo and Douglas, and it was therefore abundantly necessary for them to pretend to enjoy their own conversations. Melvyn Douglas, playing Larry Blake, publisher of a New York magazine, sees Karin, a ski instructress at a ski lodge, and promptly falls in love with her and marries her. He detests skiing, she adores it, and there is much polite banter about skis and slopes between them. "Climb this way," she says. "Spread your seat more." He asks her what they will do when they get to the top of the ski slope, and she answers in the authentic accent of Ninotchka, "We come down." Soon he wearies of the snow and returns to New York to resume his business career. His wife remains at the ski lodge until she hears that Larry has returned to the arms of his mistress, the patient Griselda. Karin flies to New York, wearing flowing garments and a curly wig, impersonating her little-known twin sister. Larry falls in love with the "twin," takes her to the ski lodge, pretends that he has known all along that there was no twin, and they set out on a wild ski chase through the snow. Larry tumbles into a pool, and as she pulls him out, he exclaims, "I'm not Larry. I'm his twin brother." Curtain.

According to the records the film had its premiere at the Capitol Theater in New York on December 31, 1941, shortly after Pearl Harbor, and was damned by the critics. It is seen occasionally on late, late shows and has lost none of its fascination as one of the most awful films ever to come out of Hollywood. The point is made in the first five minutes. Therafter it repeats the same point endlessly. It has no structure, no direction. Only rarely do we catch a glimpse of Garbo in her pride and beauty. A seduction scene seems ghoulish, as though the dead were trafficking with the dead, and there comes a time when the words "twin sister" begin to pound like pneumatic drills. Douglas kisses Garbo fourteen times. He was lucky, but deserved a happier Garbo. She was not being unduly distrustful when she thought there was a conspiracy to destroy her. *Two-faced Woman* proved to be an ironic coda to a life full of accomplishments, and she never made another film.

Curtain

After Two-faced Woman, Garbo's career as a film actress came to an end. She appeared neither on the stage nor in films, gave no interviews, made no public announcement of her intentions, and vanished from Hollywood. But the sudden end of her career was not her doing. She knew her gifts and was not prepared to surrender them easily. What happened was something so totally unexpected that it caught her by surprise. Although she was the most famous of all film actresses, and had completely mastered her craft and was therefore all the more desirable to the studios, she was unable to find a film that suited her. A hundred subjects were waiting for her. When she approached them, they shriveled up or became unmanageable. The actress went in search of a role and found nothing at all.

It was a strange situation—the roles running away from her, the plays curling up and dying as soon as she showed interest in them. At least ten, and perhaps fifteen, vehicles were considered during the next decade, but all were abandoned for reasons over which she had very little control. *Sapho*, by Alphonse Daudet, was seriously considered, with Montgomery Clift playing the romantic lover, Jean Gaussin, who falls hopelessly in love with Fanny Legrand, a woman of the world. Fanny has already ruined a string of lovers. It was a good story, but nothing came of it, perhaps because Fanny Legrand resembles a more bourgeois and more aggressive Marguerite Gautier. *Inspiration*, which she made with Robert Montgomery, had been based on Daudet's story but without acknowledgment. It was worth doing again more accurately and more honestly. The project was abandoned for no reason that anyone can remember.

Then there was Daphne du Maurier's novel *My Cousin Rachel*, which delighted Cukor so much that he made a special journey to Cornwall to meet the author of that Gothic mystery. This too fell through, perhaps because Garbo could not visualize herself as a Cornishwoman. The next was *George Sand*, which she could have played to perfection with Laurence Olivier as her leading man. It petered out like sand through an hourglass. This was followed by *The Paradine Case*, with its lethal heroine, who was more than half mad. For a while everyone at MGM was talking about it, and then almost overnight it was forgotten. RKO, which owned the rights to *I Remember Mama*, made signs to MGM hinting that it would like to borrow Cukor and Garbo for this film. The only reply from Garbo was "No murderesses, no mamas," sent by telegram.

It is possible that *I Remember Mama* was not intended as a serious suggestion. It hinted at burlesque, warmhearted and faintly obscene. No one in his senses would have seriously considered it as providing an appropriate role for Garbo. She was more interested in an adaptation of Balzac's *La Duchesse de Langeais*, a novel based on the life of another great beauty, the Marquise Henriette de Castries. Balzac fell in love with the Marquise while staying at Aix-en-Provence. She played with him like a cat playing with a mouse, but in the novel he turns the tables on her by depicting her as a coldhearted woman who is finally rejected by her lover, branded with hot irons, and thrown into a nunnery. A classic novel of a lover's revenge, written with an almost pathological cruelty, it was sufficiently dramatic to serve as a vehicle for Garbo. Walter Wanger was to be the producer, Max Ophuls the director, and James Mason was to be the lover. They had even decided upon a new title: *Friends and Lovers*. Negotiations continued over several months, Garbo signed a contract stipulating an advance payment of $50,000, costume tests were shot in color by James Wong Howe, and Garbo traveled to Italy, where the locations had already been chosen. Then quite suddenly the project was abandoned with no explanation except that Walter Wanger had failed to find sufficient financial backing. There were rumors of feuds, violent quarrels, sudden outbursts of temper, but the real reasons for the collapse of the project were never made public. In the excitement and confusion, the only color sequences ever photographed with Garbo were lost. Today they are probably moldering away in a loft in Italy.

La Duchesse de Langeais was a near miss; Max Reinhardt's *The Miracle* was wider of the mark but even more desirable. There was a period when Hollywood was abuzz with the rumor that she would play the part made famous by Lady Diana Manners, but while the rumors proliferated, no one, it appeared, had consulted Garbo. Those who remember *The Miracle* are left with the pleasant pastime of imagining Garbo in a role she would have played to perfection.

By 1949 Garbo was coming relentlessly to the conclusion that she would never make another film. It was not that she did not want to make films; it was simply that the making of films had become virtually impossible. In the past all decisions had been made by MGM. She had the right to disagree with those decisions, but she had rarely exercised this right, and she had rarely offered suggestions about the roles she would like to play. She had always felt the need to be led, to be advised, to be ordered. Also, she was totally without ambition, perhaps because ambition must have seemed preposterous to someone who had been world-famous for so long. Why struggle? Why fight? She had only to ask herself these questions to know the answer. If a film exactly suited to her dropped miraculously into her lap, she might or might not accept it. The days of her long warfare with films, which began with Mauritz Stiller and ended with George Cukor, were over. She was now free to spend her life exactly as she pleased.

Rich, famous, adored, she was in the enviable position of someone enjoying perfect freedom, and at the same time she was in the less enviable position of someone who has not the least idea how to enjoy her freedom, what to do with it, or how to spend her days. She faced the problem that confronts many people on their retirement: what can I possibly do to fill up the emptiness of the days? She was shy, hated making new friends, showed no interest in social movements, rarely glanced at a newspaper, and was strangely ill-prepared for her new life of continuous leisure.

She had almost no political consciousness. Nevertheless on two occasions she showed that she was capable of embracing political ideas. In 1938, when she was told that Hitler had seen *Camille* six times and wanted desperately to meet her, it occurred to her to accept the invitation to travel to Germany and meet the Führer with a small pistol concealed in her dress. She hoped to kill him and rid the world of its worst misery. Nothing came of the idea, but there is no doubt that she thought

about it very seriously. In the following year the Spanish Civil War came to a disastrous end. Garbo hated Franco's Nationalists passionately. The poet Edwin Rolfe, one of the survivors of the Lincoln Brigade, which fought on the side of the Republicans in Spain, has described his surprise when he returned to Hollywood and discovered that Garbo insisted on giving clothes and money to all the survivors of the brigade who reached California. She entertained them, fed them, accompanied them to the Farmer's Market, asked them interminable questions. This was her only political act. She divorced herself from politics, as gradually over the years she divorced herself from ordinary life, retreating farther and farther into silence.

It was a strange retirement. but she had chosen it for herself and found it had its own rewards. Once her career was over, she saw only the disadvantages of fame. Because it terrified her to be recognized, she wore disguises, hiding behind dark glasses and an ever renewed barrier of false names, but was nevertheless recognized whenever she walked out in the street. Those who knew her well were never surprised to hear that Miss Harriet Brown was on the telephone. Sometimes she would say absentmindedly, "I remember when I was a little boy. . . ." It was a long time ago. She had grown into middle age and then into old age so quietly that her aging can be likened to a sailing ship always moving in calm waters, very peaceful, making scarcely a ripple. She had abandoned the ordeals of Hollywood without a qualm. At the beginning of her career she had been the young and beautiful Countess Elizabeth Dohna, and at the end of her career she was the young and beautiful Ninotchka. The wheel had turned full circle. At that moment her life as an artist came to an end, and she had no regrets.

Her finest achievement was that she became a great actress, and surprisingly her best performances took place at the beginning and end of her career. Her second-finest achievement was that she refused to take her own legend seriously. She was modest about her gifts, which were very great.

In this outrageous and corrupt age, with dictators and armies continually on the rampage, Garbo came as a benediction, reminding us that there existed in the world the perfect beauty we had all been seeking. She seemed in our imaginations to be walking among us like a goddess, and we saw in her beauty the promise of an unhoped-for peace.

We live in a dark age, but she was all brightness. Her beauty was not simply a very appealing arrangement of planes and surfaces: It was charged with energy. It was a beauty that sprang at us and took us by the throat, and did not let us rest; and if it seemed peaceful, this too was an illusion, for a saving energy poured out of her to revive us and heal our wounds. So Athena must have appeared to the ancient Greeks and Nefertiti to the ancient Egyptians.

In just the same way in the face of the Buddha, as it has been sculptured in stone and bronze in India and all over the Far East, we are aware of a great peace that is also power. The serenity of the Buddha image conceals the lightning and the thunder, the doom of kingdoms, the creation of worlds. He is not merely meditating. He is giving of himself in fierce abundance, though his eyes are half closed and his hands are folded on his lap and he smiles softly. And if he is shaped beautifully, it is only in order to make him more comprehensible to us. There are in fact smooth Cambodian images of the Buddha that look remarkably like Garbo: vivid, powerful, utterly peaceful, with the same energy streaming from their faces.

Future generations may envy us, for we saw her in her own time. They, too, will wonder at the mysteries surrounding her—those mysteries that were conjured up on the day when the forgotten genius Mauritz Stiller, out of the misery of his haunted childhood, imagined he saw someone—goddess or snow maiden—so beautiful that she could scarcely be believed, and called her Garbo.

Hollywood–New York
1951–1976

Acknowledgments

I am deeply indebted to Ivy Wilson, Melvyn Douglas, George Cukor, and Rexford Stead, who talked to me about Garbo and let me talk to them; and to Mr. Homler of the MGM still department, who let me loose among a hundred thousand stills.

I am indebted to the Svenska Filminstitutet of Stockholm for the photographs on pages 28, 37, 44, 49, 50, 52, 65, and 73, and to the Museum of Modern Art for those on pages 24, 46, 60, 63, 67, 70, 80, 83, 88, 95, 98, 170, 199, and 255. I would like to thank William Rayner of Condé Nast Publications for permission to use the photograph by Arnold Genthe that appears on page 101 and Lena Daun of the Swedish Information Service of New York for the photograph of Mauritz Stiller that appears on page 56.

For helping me to find photographs, I am grateful to Cinemabilia of New York, which contributed the photograph on page 16, and to *Movie Star News* of New York. Also, the Motion Picture Academy's librarians were always kindly and helpful.

Chronology

1871	May 11	Karl Alfrid Gustafsson born
1872	September 10	Anna Lovisa Karlsson born
1883	July 17	Mauritz Stiller born
1905	September 18	Greta Lovisa Gustafsson born
1912	August 22	She enters Catherina School
1919	June 14	She leaves school
1920	June 1	Karl Gustafsson dies
	June 13	Greta's first Communion
	July 26	She applies for job at PUB
1922	July 22	She leaves PUB
	September 18	She registers at Royal Dramatic Academy
	December 26	Premiere of *Luffar-Petter*
1923	July 23	She signs contract with Stiller
	Fall	Production of *Gösta Berlings Saga* begins
	November 9	She changes her name to Greta Garbo

1924	March 10 and 17	Premiere of *Gösta Berlings Saga*
	Fall	She travels to Constantinople and returns to Berlin to work on *The Street of Sorrows*
	Late November	She meets Louis B. Mayer in Berlin
1925	May 18	Premiere of *The Street of Sorrows* in Berlin
	July 6	She arrives with Stiller in New York
1926	February 8	*The Torrent* released
	October 3	*The Temptress* released
1927	January 9	*Flesh and the Devil* released
	November 29	*Love* released
1928	January 14	*The Divine Woman* released
	August 4	*The Mysterious Lady* released
	November 8	Mauritz Stiller dies in Stockholm
1929	January 19	*A Woman of Affairs* released
	March 9	Garbo sails from New York to Gothenburg
	March 30	*Wild Orchids* released
	July 27	*The Single Standard* released
	November 16	*The Kiss* released
1930	March 14	*Anna Christie* released
	August 22	*Romance* released
1931	February 6	*Inspiration* released
	October 16	*Susan Lenox: Her Fall and Rise* released
	December 31	*Mata Hari* released
1932	April 12	*Grand Hotel* released
	June 1	Her contract with MGM terminates, and she goes to Sweden for eight months
	June 2	*As You Desire Me* released
1933	December 26	*Queen Christina* released
1934	December 7	*The Painted Veil* released
1935	August 30	*Anna Karenina* released
1936	January 9	John Gilbert dies
	September 14	Irving Thalberg dies
	December 30	Garbo receives Sweden's highest award for the arts: the medal *Literis et artibus*
1937	January 22	*Camille* released
	November 4	*Conquest* released
1939	November 9	*Ninotchka* released
1941	December 31	*Two-faced Woman* released

Bibliography

BACHMANN, GIDEON (ed.). *Six Talks on G. W. Pabst*. New York: The Group for Film Study, 1955.

BAINBRIDGE, JOHN. *Garbo*. New York: Galahad Books, 1974.

BEHLMER, RUDY (ed.). *Memo from David O. Selznick*. New York: Viking Press, 1972.

BEHRMAN, S. N. *People in a Diary*. Boston: Little, Brown, 1972.

BILLQUIST, FRITIOF. *Garbo: A Biography*. New York: G. P. Putnam's Sons, 1960.

CAREY, GARY. *Cukor & Co*. New York: Museum of Modern Art, 1971.

CONWAY, MICHAEL. *The Films of Greta Garbo*. New York: Bonanza Books, 1963.

COOKE, ALISTAIR. *Garbo and the Night Watchman*. New York: McGraw-Hill, 1971.

CORLISS, RICHARD. *Greta Garbo*. New York: Pyramid, 1974.

CROWTHER, BOSLEY. *Hollywood Rajah*. New York: Dell, 1961.

CUTTS, JOHN. *"Ninotchka," Films and Filming*, March 1962.

DUMAS, ALEXANDRE. *Camille*. New York: Heritage Press, 1955.

DURGNAT, RAYMOND, and JOHN KOBAL. *Greta Garbo*. New York: E. P. Dutton, 1965.

GENTHE, ARNOLD. *As I Remember*. New York: Reynal & Hitchcock, 1936.

GOLDSMITH, MARGARET. *Christina of Sweden*. New York: Doubleday, Doran, 1935.

HARDY, FORSYTH. *Scandinavian Film*. London: Falcon Press, 1952.

LAING, E. E. *Greta Garbo: The Story of a Specialist*. London: John Gifford, 1946.

LAMBERT, GAVIN. *On Cukor*. New York: G. P. Putnam's Sons, 1972.

MARION, FRANCES. *Off with Their Heads!* New York: Macmillan, 1972.

PALMBORG, RILLA PAGE. *The Private Life of Greta Garbo*. New York: Doubleday, Doran, 1931.

PENSEL, HANS. *Seastrom and Stiller in Hollywood*. New York: Vantage Press, 1969.

ROTHA, PAUL. *The Film till Now*. London: Vision Press, 1949.

SARRIS, ANDREW. *Interviews with Film Directors*. New York: Discus Books, 1967.

SIEGEL, JOEL E. *Val Lewton: The Reality of Terror*. New York: Viking Press, 1973.

SJOLANDER, TURE. *Garbo*. New York: Harper & Row, 1973.

TYLER, PARKER. *Classics of the Silent Film*. New York: Citadel Press, 1962.

WHITEHALL, RICHARD. *"Garbo: How Good Was She?" Film and Filming*, September 1963.

Index

293

OTHER
COOPER SQUARE PRESS
TITLES OF INTEREST

JUDY GARLAND
The Day-By-Day Chronicle of a Legend
Scott Schechter
416 pp., 80 b/w photos
0-8154-1205-3
$26.95 cloth

THE RUNAWAY BRIDE
Hollywood Romantic Comedy
of the 1930s
Elizabeth Kendall
312 pp., 24 b/w photos
0-8154-1199-5
$18.95

HOLLYWOOD REMEMBERED
An Oral History of Its Golden Age
Paul Zollo
416 pp., 43 b/w photos, 1 map
0-8154-1239-8
$27.95 cloth

A SILENT SIREN SONG
The Aitken Brothers' Hollywood
Odyssey, 1905–1926
Al P. Nelson and Mel R. Jones
288 pp., 42 b/w photos
0-8154-1069-7
$25.95 cloth

MY STORY
Marilyn Monroe
Co-authored by Ben Hecht
New introduction by
Andrea Dworkin
152 pp., 4 color photos,
14 b/w photos
0-8154-1102-2
$22.95 cloth

BLUE ANGEL
The Life of Marlene Dietrich
Donald Spoto
374 pp., 58 b/w photos
0-8154-1061-1
$18.95

THE BOYS FROM SYRACUSE
The Shuberts' Theatrical Empire
Foster Hirsch
374 pp., 24 b/w photos
0-8154-1103-0
$18.95

CLARA BOW
Runnin' Wild
David Stenn
with a new filmography
368 pp., 27 b/w photos
0-8154-1025-5
$21.95

FRANCOIS TRUFFAUT
Correspondence, 1945–1984
Edited by Gilles Jacob and
Claude de Givray
Foreword by
Jean-Luc Godard
608 pp., 81 b/w photos,
drawings, and facsimiles
0-8154-1024-7
$24.95

FILM CULTURE READER
Edited by P. Adams Sitney
464 pp., 80 b/w illustrations
0-8154-1101-4
$18.95

CONVERSATIONS WITH BRANDO
Lawrence Grobel
with a new afterword
238 pp., 17 b/w photos
0-8154-1014-X
$15.95

BETTY GARRETT AND OTHER SONGS
A Life on Stage and Screen
Betty Garrett with
Ron Rapoport
306 pp., 52 b/w photos
1-56833-098-7 (cloth);
1-56833-133-9 (paperback)
$23.95 (cloth); $18.95
(paperback)
Madison Books

LON CHANEY
The Man behind the
Thousand Faces
Michael F. Blake
408 pp., 110 b/w photos
1-879511-09-6
$19.95
Madison Books

MY LIFE IS IN YOUR HANDS & TAKE MY LIFE
The Autobiographies of Eddie Cantor
Eddie Cantor with David
Freedman/Jane Kesner
Ardmore
Foreword by Will Rogers
New Introduction by
Leonard Maltin
650 pp., 63 b/w photos
0-8154-1057-3
$25.95

LOU'S ON FIRST
A Biography of Lou Costello
Chris Costello with
Raymond Strait
288 pp., 31 b/w photos
0-8154-1073-2
$17.95

LAURENCE OLIVIER
A Biography
Donald Spoto
528 pp., 110 b/w photos
0-8154-1146-4
$21.95

REBEL
The Life and Legend of James Dean
Donald Spoto
352 pp., 41 b/w illustrations
0-8154-1071-9
$18.95

GARY COOPER
American Hero
Jeffrey Meyers
404 pp., 32 b/w photos
0-8154-1140-5
$18.95

THE HUSTONS
The Life and Times of a
Hollywood Dynasty
Updated Edition
Lawrence Grobel
872 pp., 61 b/w photos
0-8154-1026-3
$29.95

THE LAST LAUGH
The World of Stand-Up Comics
Updated Edition
Phil Berger
464 pp., 38 b/w photos
0-8154-1096-4
$18.95

I, FELLINI
Charlotte Chandler
Foreword by Billy Wilder
448 pp., 51 b/w photos
0-8154-1143-X
$19.95

HOLY TERROR
Andy Warhol Close Up
Bob Colacello
560 pp., 74 b/w photos
0-8154-1008-5
$17.95

THE UNRULY LIFE OF WOODY ALLEN
A Biography
Marion Meade
384 pp., 26 b/w photos
0-8154-1149-9
$18.95

MARILYN MONROE
The Biography
Donald Spoto
752 pp., 50 b/w photos
0-8154-1183-9
$24.95

REMINISCING WITH NOBLE SISSLE
AND EUBIE BLAKE
Robert Kimball and William
Bolcom
256 pp., 244 b/w photos
0-8154-1045-X
$24.95

STEPS IN TIME
Fred Astaire
Foreword by Ginger Rogers
New introduction by
Jennifer Dunning
376 pp., 46 b/w photos
0-8154-1058-1
$19.95

CONVERSATIONS WITH BRANDO
Lawrence Grobel
with a new afterword
238 pp., 17 b/w photos
0-8154-1014-X
$15.95

BLACKFACE
Reflections on African
Americans in the Movies
Expanded Edition
Nelson George
330 pp., 23 b/w photos
0-8154-1194-4
$16.95

Available at bookstores
or call 1-800-462-6420

 Cooper Square Press

200 Park Avenue South ◆ Suite 1109 ◆ New York, New York
10003
www.coopersquarepress.com